Discover the Power Within Yourself

Psychic vampirism is alive and flourishing in the world today. Whether one-on-one, group, parasitic, or global in form, psychic vampirism exacts a heavy toll—it demands energy, and in some instances, destroys lives. At a personal level, it wastes our energies and interrupts our growth. At a global level, it can literally drain the earth of its survival resources.

This book precisely identifies the underlying dynamics of this widespread phenomenon. It develops step-by-step strategies to confront and overcome psychic vampirism in whatever form it takes. With this book, you can discover the power within yourself to ward off psychic attacks, and to protect and replenish your life-force energy.

About the Author

Joe H. Slate, Ph.D. (Alabama) is a licensed psychologist in private practice. His extensive academic background led to his pioneering research on altered states and psychic processes. He is the author of *Psychic Empowerment, Psychic Empowerment for Health and Fitness, Astral Projection and Psychic Empowerment, Aura Energy for Health, Healing & Balance,* and *Rejuvenation: Strategies for Living Younger, Longer & Better.*

To Write to the Author

If you wish to contact the author, or would like more information about this book, please write to the author in care of Llewellyn Worldwide, and we will forward your request. Both the author and the publisher appreciate hearing from you and learning of your enjoyment of this book and how it has helped you. Llewellyn Worldwide cannot guarantee that every letter written to the author can be answered, but all will be forwarded. Please write to:

Joe H. Slate, Ph.D.
℅ Llewellyn Worldwide
2143 Wooddale Drive
Woodbury, MN 55125-2989

Please enclose a self-addressed, stamped envelope for reply, or $1.00 to cover costs. If outside the U.S.A., enclose international postal reply coupon.

Many of Llewellyn's authors have websites with additional information and resources. For more information, please visit our website at:

www.llewellyn.com

PSYCHIC VAMPIRES

Protection from
Energy Predators & Parasites

JOE H. SLATE, Ph.D.

Llewellyn Publications
Woodbury, Minnesota

FIRST EDITION
Fifteenth Printing, 2024

Book design and editing: Michael Maupin
Cover design: Gavin Dayton Duffy
Photographs courtesy of Joe H. Slate

Library of Congress Cataloging-in-Publication Data
Slate, Joe H.
    Psychic Vampires : protection from energy predators & parasites /
        Joe H. Slate.—1st ed.
            p.   cm.
    Includes bibliographical references and index.
    ISBN 13: 978-0-7387-0191-2
    ISBN 10: 0-7387-0191-2

    1. Self-defense—Psychic aspects. 2. Vital force. 3. Vampires—Psychology.
        I. Title.

BF1045.S46 S53 2002
133.8—dc21   2001050842

Llewellyn Publications
A Division of Llewellyn Worldwide Ltd.
2143 Woodale Drive
Woodbury, MN 55125-2989
Llewellyn is a registered trademark of Llewellyn Worldwide Ltd.
Printed in the United States of America.

Other Books by Joe H. Slate

Psychic Empowerment

Psychic Empowerment for Health and Fitness

Astral Projection and Psychic Empowerment

Aura Energy for Health, Healing & Balance

Rejuvenation

Beyond Reincarnation

Connecting to the Power of Nature

With Carl Llewellyn Weschcke

Psychic Empowerment for Everyone

Psychic Empowerment Tools & Techniques for Growth & Transformation

Self-Empowerment and Your Subconscious Mind

Self-Empowerment through Self-Hypnosis

Astral Projection for Psychic Empowerment

Clairvoyance for Psychic Empowerment

Doors to Past Lives & Future Lives

The Llewellyn Complete Book of Psychic Empowerment

Contents

List of Figures

Acknowledgments

THIS BOOK HAS grown out of years of research and collaboration with my many learned colleagues who are firmly committed to the search for new knowledge. For their invaluable contributions to this project, I owe an enormous debt of gratitude.

Also, to the many students who contributed to my studies of psychic vampirism, I am especially indebted. To the research assistants who helped plan and organize experimental studies as well as gather and process research data, I will always be grateful. They were more than research assistants—they were an invaluable source of inspiration and intellectual stimulation. Many of their creative ideas found their way first into the research laboratory and from there into the pages of this book.

Very special thanks are due the many research subjects, including both students and nonstudents, who volunteered to participate in my studies. They are the heart of this book—without their cooperation, this effort could not have been completed.

Finally, to the men and women at Llewellyn Publications, I here express my sincerest appreciation for their interest in my work, and beyond that, for their commitment toward discovering and advancing "new worlds of mind and spirit."

Preface

UP UNTIL NOW, vampires of the psychic kind, not unlike their fictional counterparts, were generally thought to be menacing creatures of the dark who were driven by a repulsive, sinister force that demanded the exploitation and wanton seduction of unsuspecting host victims. As consumers of energy rather than blood, they were seen as stealthily attacking the energy system of others in a devious effort to satisfy their insatiable drive. Unfortunately, such a narrow, stereotypical view seriously constricted our understanding of psychic vampirism and thwarted our efforts to master workable empowerment strategies related to this widespread, highly complex phenomenon.

This book offers a totally new approach to the study of psychic vampirism. It examines psychic vampirism in its various forms—from individual to global—with emphasis on objective, practical strategies that are both enlightening and empowering. It views psychic vampirism as multidimensional with mental, physical, and spiritual components, each of which is critical to our understanding of this often misunderstood phenomenon. It explores the environmental, developmental, and past-life factors associated with psychic vampirism, and incorporates them into sensible, step-by-step empowerment procedures that can be used by everyone.

The term *psychic vampirism* as used in this book denotes the condition and practice of being a psychic vampire, as well as concepts associated with the various forms of this phenomenon. In my treatment of this topic, I have carefully avoided a narrow, judgmental perspective of psychic vampirism, preferring instead a more functional, objective approach that explains the phenomenon and develops productive ways of encountering it. Because psychic vampirism is essentially an energy phenomenon, my treatment of this important topic focuses on not one but two interactive life-force energy systems—the one within the self and the other in the higher cosmos. Awareness of these two critical systems, along with ways to interconnect them, is essential to our mastery of vampire-related empowerment and protection strategies. Even psychic vampires can be liberated and empowered through procedures that unblock the flow of life-force energy by linking the internal energy system to the higher cosmic system.

Among my major objectives in writing this book is the exploration of certain forms of psychic vampirism either previously unknown or, until now, largely ignored. Among the examples are group vampirism, which can involve organized vampire efforts of large numbers of persons including predator corporations and institutions; parasitic vampirism, in which an inner vampire state feeds on the self's internal energy resources; and global vampirism, in which certain widespread global conditions erode the human potential for growth and global progress. In each of its forms, psychic vampirism can be so common that we overlook it, or else forget it is there. Unfortunately, whenever psychic vampirism is rampant in one form, it is usually pervasive in other forms too.

The empowerment techniques presented in this book range from such proven basics as visualization and affirmations to the use of various altered states and tangible psychic tools. Each strategy, along with the Seven-Day Psychic Protection Plan found at the end of the book, recognizes two essential principles: first, the incomparable worth of all human beings; and second, the human potential for growth and greatness. Together, these interrelated principles form the book's centerpiece and each empowerment procedure presented in it.

ONE

Psychic Vampirism:
A Comprehensive View

MY INTEREST IN psychic vampirism began over twenty-five years ago when I received a research contract to study the human energy system from a seemingly unlikely source—the U.S. Army Missile Research and Development Command. Although the purpose of the project was to investigate the energy field enveloping the human body, it became increasingly evident during the thirteen-month study that the body's external energy field, commonly called the *human aura,* is but an outward manifestation of a dynamic internal energy system. Conducted at Athens State College (now University), the study, along with several follow-up projects, found the human energy system to be a highly sensitive, complex phenomenon that is affected by the mental and physical state of the individual as well as a host of external factors. Of particular relevance to the system are a variety of social influences, including our interactions with other human energy systems.

Taken together, the evidence is clear—the human energy system, with its complex structure and functions, is flawlessly engineered to energize and sustain our existence as an indestructible life-force entity. It transcends biology in essence, function, and design. Without question, the deeper our understanding of that energy system and the forces that affect it, the richer the quality of our present lives and the greater our potential for future growth.

Exquisitely designed, the human energy system is flexible and developmental in nature. Figuring out ways to empower that system and promote its evolvement is one of our greatest challenges. We now know that the human energy system is responsive to the same conditions that enrich our overall growth, such as an enriched environment, a positive self-image, a sense of well-being, and a state of inner balance. Similarly, the conditions that impair our total growth likewise impair the energy system and its functions.

Psychic vampirism is a widespread yet often unrecognized human energy phenomenon that can interrupt our growth and impede our progress. As already noted, it exists in a variety of forms, each of which subtly consumes its victim's energy and over the long haul, erodes the energy system itself. Although no known force can totally destroy the human energy system because of its cosmic makeup, psychic vampirism can impair its functions and seriously damage its capacity to energize growth. Consequently, understanding psychic vampirism and, equally as important, mastering the psychic empowerment strategies related to it are critical in our struggle to realize our growth potentials and achieve our highest level of self-fulfillment.

Although psychic vampirism exists in various forms, the expression, unless qualified, typically denotes psychic vampirism between two persons, the one being the psychic vampire and the other the host victim. In that context, the psychic vampire, who is deficient in energy resources, taps the energy reserve of a host victim for the express purpose of extracting energy from it. The immediate effects vary but usually include a new surge of revitalizing energy for the psychic vampire and a critical depletion of essential energy for the vampirized victim.

Unfortunately, the long-term consequences of recurring vampire assaults on the energy system can be extremely harmful, not only for the host victim but for the psychic vampire as well. Short-circuiting the internal energy system sabotages the psychic vampire's personal development, thus arresting healthy development and making repeated vampire interactions necessary. The host victim's energy system, on the other hand, becomes stressed by the depletion of energy and overworked in order to generate new energy. Given recurrent attacks, the victim's energy supply can become chronically depleted and the internal energy system itself can become severely damaged.

While psychic vampirism between two persons is widespread, it exists, as already noted, in a variety of other forms, some of which are explored in depth for the first time in this book. Included are several types of self-contained or *parasitic vampirism,* which is vampirism turned inwardly, along with *group vampirism,* a collective form of social psychic vampirism which is often found among informal groups as well as structured organizations and institutions. As we will later see, the different forms of psychic vampirism are in some ways similar; however the tactics used by psychic vampires vary widely, depending largely on the type of vampirism and the setting in which it occurs.

My major purpose in writing this book is two-fold: first, to promote a better understanding of contemporary psychic vampirism in its multiple forms; and second, to offer relevant strategies which can be used by everyone to take decisive command of any psychic vampire situation. To achieve these goals, we will first examine the roots of contemporary psychic vampirism—including fiction and folklore. We will then look at the human energy system and explore its relevance to psychic vampirism. Next, we will explore ways of identifying psychic vampirism and explaining the different manifestations of this interesting but menacing phenomenon. We will present totally new step-by-step procedures for counteracting psychic vampirism and protecting oneself against it. We will also offer highly specific procedures that can be used by the psychic vampire to overcome the vampire impulse and reverse its self-defeating effects.

The concepts and strategies presented throughout this book are based, not on theory or speculation, but on controlled laboratory experiments conducted in the college setting over the past quarter century by the author with the assistance of students and researchers from various disciplines. Admittedly, our studies of psychic vampirism have raised many important questions yet to be answered. Nevertheless, we finally know enough about this complex phenomenon not only to identify it when it occurs, but also to take immediate, decisive action to confront and overcome it.

Fictional and Folklore Roots

Psychic vampirism has a long and colorful history that embraces contributions of both fiction and folklore. Throughout history, fictional concepts were often the forerunners for important cultural progress. They found their way into our culture because they contributed in some way to our understanding of ourselves and the world around us. Science fiction, in particular, has repeatedly exploded the conventional envelope by generating highly creative concepts and even detailed designs that led to new knowledge and major advancements in science and technology. A striking example is biometrics. First introduced as fiction, various biometric strategies, including electro-sensory recordings and iris scans, are now routinely used in many security settings for identification purposes. The recent breaking of the human genetic code is an even more striking example of how science fiction introduced new concepts and technologies that fueled later scientific advancements.

Equally as important as the contributions of science fiction to cultural progress are the imaginative myths and legends that introduced many basic elements considered relevant to our contemporary understanding of human behavior. Included are the many concepts based on Greek mythology that found their way, first into psychoanalysis and then into mainstream thinking. Among the familiar examples are the Oedipus and Electra complexes, which represent respectively the male and female child's attraction to parent of the other sex. According to many contemporary child development specialists, these complexes if unresolved can generate serious growth obstacles and later adjustment problems in adolescence and adulthood. Our studies found, in fact, that psychic vampirism is often associated with unresolved Oedipus or Electra strivings. It could be argued, of course, that the psychic struggles illustrated by Greek mythology existed as common cultural realities long before any mythological or fictional treatment of them. Nevertheless, mythology gave substance and relevance to them. By providing colorful examples of fundamental human conflicts, mythology increased our awareness and understanding of them, a contribution recognized by the descriptive terms still in use today.

Given the many invaluable contributions of fiction and mythology to our present-day understanding of human behavior, it is not surprising that fictional and folklore vampirism would emerge as a relevant forerunner to its real-life counterpart—psychic vampirism.

According to ancient folklore, vampires were undead creatures of the dark who left their tombs at night to suck blood from the living through puncture wounds inflicted by sharp incisor teeth, the vampire's weapon of choice. A pair of puncture wounds, particularly to the neck region, provided telltale evidence of a recent vampire attack.

Once infused with a fresh supply of blood, the emboldened vampire became temporarily energized while the unfortunate victim, enfeebled by the loss of blood, became increasingly vulnerable to future attacks. In the worst scenario, the victim became a reluctant vampire who, in turn, preyed upon others, thus perpetuating the vampire's dark chain of anguish. The more fiendish and advanced vampires were believed to possess powers so great that they could at will take on the physical form of a wild animal, particular a wolf or bat.

As the colorful thread of vampire folklore progressively found its way into the fabric of various cultures, vampirism as the embodiment of horror assumed a highly significant literary role. After several early writers, including Philostratus and Phlegon of Tralles, wrote on the topic, the insatiable vampire became the subject of many notable works, among them Goethe's *Braut von Korinth* and Giovanni Polidori's *The Vampyre* (1819). Of particular importance was Polidori's work, which became the source of a nineteenth-century French melodrama as well as two important German operas, *Der Vampyre*, both produced in 1828.

It was, however, Bram Stoker's fascinating and wildly popular *Dracula* (1897) that captivated readers everywhere. Dramatized and produced for the first time by John Balderston and Hamilton Deane in 1927, the spectacular novel not only generated enormous interest in vampirism, it brought world fame to the bloodthirsty despot of Transylvania. In recent years, a deluge of books and TV dramas, along with several blockbuster movies starring seasoned actors as well as hot newcomers, stirred greater interest in vampirism and, in particular, the ruthless Dracula. Timeless in its appeal, the classic Dracula legend continues to hit a global nerve—thanks not only to the universal relevance of its underlying themes, but also because of captivating moviemaking with extraordinary power to connect generations.

As it turns out, much of the Dracula legend is based on historical fact, its real-life source being that of the notorious Romanian prince, Vlad Dracula (1431–1476), who became known as Vlad the Impaler for executing his enemies by hoisting them on stakes for a slow, agonizing death. From his Transylvanian castle in the rugged mountainous region of Romania, the infamous Dracula reportedly ordered and actively participated in the torture and death of countless unfortunate victims, including scores of his own subjects. Though the accounts of Dracula's life are sketchy, his reign of terror apparently ended violently in 1476 when, according to legend, he was assassinated and beheaded by his political enemies.

But in all fairness to Dracula, his place in history as an icon of evil, having only moderate historical support, may be somewhat ill deserved. According to many contemporary historians, the dubious accounts of Dracula's atrocities are more than counterbalanced by his accomplishments. For instance, he boldly warded off the Turkish invasion of Romania, thereby actually saving the country and preventing the death of thousands. Even today, Transylvania continues to benefit from the world-famous nobleman who is recognized by many Romanians as a national hero rather than a heartless villain. Now at an all-time high, tourism in Transylvania, including vampire fests, conferences, seminars, workshops, and other events commemorating Dracula, has bolstered the troubled economy by sharply increasing revenue. In fact, contemporary interest in Dracula is so great that a Dracula Land theme park to be located at the birthplace of the legendary count is now being planned by the Romanian government. (As an interesting footnote, it was directly over Transylvania during a Dracula vampire fest that the 1999 eclipse of the sun, one of nature's most beautiful and awe-inspiring events, reached the perfect peak of its brief total phase.)

As typically depicted in folklore, literature, and horror films, legendary vampires are clever creatures of the dark who sleep during the daylight hours in a crypt and roam the streets and countryside at night in search of prey from whom to siphon life-sustaining blood. Typically clad in a black cape with deep-red lining, vampires as a general rule display a suave sense of entitlement, and they expect naked compliance to their demands. Generally shrewd and seductive, they cleverly orchestrate situations and arrogantly manipulate their innocent, vulnerable prey. As shadowy, complex creatures, they can shift with ease from engaging charm to callous control. Their gaze can be at once piercing and seductive, and their speech calculated and mesmerizing. As icy icons of evil, they typically generate in others an uneasy admixture of attraction, vulnerability, and fear. Almost never do they show compassion for their unfortunate victims or remorse for their ruthless conquests. In certain rare instances, the host victim is an animal, but only for the highly inexperienced, blood-deprived vampire.

The legendary vampire's extraordinary powers seem to have almost no limits. They can defy gravity by levitating and remaining suspended in mid-air, flying over buildings, floating in and out of windows, crawling up or down walls, and slithering across ceilings. They can on demand appear instantly out of thin air, and turn abruptly into a vaporous mist. They can communicate mentally, see into the future, and observe distant happenings as they occur. They reflect no image in a mirror, and although they cast no shadow, they have power to become themselves a shadow. In the crypt, they can assume a complete state of suspended animation, thus extinguishing all physical signs of life.

As supernatural beings, fictional vampires discovered early on the secrets of rejuvenation and longevity. Given the power to effectively arrest and even reverse the aging process, they in fact almost mastered the art of living forever. With critical physiological functions under their control, illness and biological erosion are unknown to them, provided their life-sustaining blood-needs are met. Although they are repelled by garlic and certain religious objects, only direct sunlight or a wooden stake driven through the heart is fatal to them, at least in terminating their physical existence. More extreme procedures, however, are required to ensure total, irrevocable death of the vampire spirit—the vampire's head must be severed from the body, and equally as important, the heart must be cut out and burned. Finally, the vampire's head must be buried at a considerable distance away from the body, and the heart's ashes must be strewn over a large, remote area. Without these extreme measures, the vampire can survive in reanimated, undead human form.

In recent years, movies of both the horror and comedy genres placed the vampire in a variety of present-day settings, a strategy that dramatically increased the legend's contemporary appeal. In horror movies, vampires are often seen crouched in the shadows, or stealthily stalking their victims, then suddenly pouncing upon them to drain blood from their bodies through puncture wounds to the neck. Unfettered by old stereotypes, modern versions of the vampire include both men and women, teens and adults, laborers in hard hats, professionals in business suits, and more recently, wealthy dot.comers. Ranging from the dapper CEO to the genial all-American cowboy, contemporary bloodsucking vampires in high-scare movies are almost always depicted as nefarious yet conflicted predators of innocent, unsuspecting victims.

Like vampire movies of the horror genre, treatment of the vampire legend as comedy entertainment found a highly receptive audience. By infusing humor into the legend, creepy comedy created very likable vampires who were at once bizarre and delightfully seductive, but scarcely dangerous. The vampire as a celebrated icon of both horror and comedy entertainment proved so incredibly popular that it was eventually enshrined on the U.S. postage stamp to the delight of vampire fans everywhere. From vampire video games for children to college-level courses on vampire literature, the vampire legend in our culture today is indeed alive and well.

Having gained expansive recognition as a model of malevolence, the legendary vampire may have inadvertently provided the seminal inspiration for its benevolent counterparts, those exemplary champions of justice—Batman and Superman—who, incidentally, also donned capes and defied gravity. As reigning paragons of good rather than evil, their struggles were equally as intense as the vampire's; and like the vampire, they adapted with ease to cultural trends, shifts, and mutations.

The enduring popularity of vampirism in both literature and entertainment media may be due, at least in part, to the universal relevance and appeal of its underlying themes—good versus evil, hope versus despair, and of course, life versus death. Disconcerting as it may be, the vampire's struggle for survival and significance is so much like our own, that the vampire has become a dominant archetype in cultures around the world. A parasite feeding on the blood of the living, this enigmatic undead creature is thoroughly instilled in our global consciousness as the consummate blend of intrigue, indulgence, and immortality.

Psychic Vampirism

Vampirism of the psychic kind, like its fictional counterpart, has a long and intriguing history. There is, in fact, considerable evidence to suggest that psychic vampirism in its various forms long predated the popular folklore versions of vampirism. Thus, the psychic vampire could be seen as the actual forerunner of its fictional com-peer, rather than vice versa. It is, in fact, strongly plausible that the widespread existence of vampirism in its psychic form actually gave rise to the folklore notion of vampires as blood-sucking rather than energy-sucking beings. From a purely chronological perspective, our study of vampirism could have quite reasonably begun with a consideration of psychic rather than fictional vampirism.

Supportive of psychic vampirism as the precursor of its folklore counterpart are the many primitive tribal rites and warlike practices that contained unmistakable traces of psychic vampirism. Many tribal prebattle rituals, for instance, were designed specifically to render enemy forces powerless by draining them of their energy and prowess. Also, the use of masks and war paint were common tribal strategies used not only to embolden the warriors but to enfeeble and disarm their opponents, thus vampirizing them primarily through intimidation and fear.

Along another line, several Biblical accounts strongly suggest psy-chic vampirism or at least variations of it. A familiar example is Del-ilah's cunning seduction of Samson. By cutting Samson's hair—the source of his energy—as he slept, she drained him of his strength and rendered him helpless before his enemies, the Philistines. Delilah in turn was apparently energized by the whole affair, thus completing the vampire transaction. Another interesting Biblical account with strong hints of psychic vampirism is Christ's description of scribes and Pharisees as vipers and serpents, "full of extortion and excess." They were accused of devouring houses and binding upon others "heavy burdens, grievous to the bone," clear fingerprints of psychic vampirism with a ravenous appetite for harming others.

Along a totally different line, numerous Biblical accounts suggest energy phenomena similar in dynamics to psychic vampirism but with effects that were the direct opposites. A familiar example are the incidents depicted in a Biblical version of creation in which God first created Adam from dust and then infused him with the breath (ener-gies) of life. A rib (of energy) was then removed from Adam to create Eve. Endowed with life-force energy, Adam and Eve became "living souls"—that is, they were cosmically energized. Another example involves Moses who, upon coming down from Mount Sinai with two tablets of stone, glowed with a new infusion of cosmic energy. In yet another instance, a woman who, upon touching the hem of Christ's garment, experienced a new infusion of energy while Christ simultaneously felt the energy leave his body. Today, phenomena such as psychic and spiritual healing are often explained as a transfer of healing energy from an energy source to a recipient.

While the empowering transfer of energy is a far cry from psychic vampirism, the underlying dynamics are strikingly similar. Energy, by nature, is fluid and transferable. This is illustrated in physics by the principles of entropy and equivalence in which two unequally charged bodies, when placed in close proximity, tend to give off and receive energy until both reach a state of equivalence. Psychic vampirism can be seen as a variation of that spontaneous process in that one body of energy (the psychic vampire) encroaches upon another body of energy (the victim), typically when in close proximity, for the express purpose of forcefully extracting energy from it.

Explaining Psychic Vampirism

Like most human behaviors, psychic vampirism can be explained from a variety of perspectives, each of which can help us to better understand this complex phenomenon. While the perspectives that follow focus primarily on psychic vampirism between two persons, they have implications for other forms as well.

One rather simplistic view holds that psychic vampirism is basically instinctual, a built-in component of a larger drive to survive. As such, it is essentially beyond our control—all efforts to alter or extinguish it are, for the most part, futile. This pessimistic view fails to note, however, that psychic vampirism, unlike instincts, usually develops gradually, thus offering ample opportunity for corrective intervention anywhere along the way.

Another view of psychic vampirism holds that we are first and foremost biological beings who are driven by certain basic physical drives—hunger, thirst, sex, sleep, activity, comfort, and energy. Here, psychic vampirism is explained simply as a means to an end—it's a way of satisfying the human need for energy. Individual differences, past experiences, and unique personal characteristics are seen as relatively unimportant. A major contribution of this perspective is its recognition of energy as a basic human drive; its major limitation is a failure to recognize the critical importance of responsible choice and self-determination in satisfying that drive.

Another view of psychic vampirism is based on the concept that seeking pleasure while avoiding pain is the major motivational force underlying human behavior. From this perspective, psychic vampirism is a raw, untamed drive that demands instant pleasure and gratification. It is easier and more pleasurable to tap the energy supply of another person than to develop one's own energy system. This limited perspective opens the floodgates for psychic vampirism to develop as a controlling force in our lives. Like the other perspectives discussed, it minimizes our capacity to take command of our personal growth and shape our own destiny.

Psychic vampirism also focuses on the social nature of our makeup. In this perspective, we interact with individuals and groups that are consistent with our roles and needs as social beings. Typically, when we give something to the relationship we expect to gain something in return. Ideally, social interactions are mutually satisfying with everyone getting a fair return; however, the investments and rewards of many human relationships are unequal. In psychic vampirism, the interaction is reduced to a calculated, unbalanced encounter in which the vampire benefits and the victim loses. A limitation of this perspective is its tendency to minimize the importance of influences beyond the social situation, including individual differences in values, predispositions, and interests.

Another perspective of psychic vampirism emphasizes perception as the major determinant of human behavior, and that psychic vampires are victims of their own perceptions. They engage in vampire behaviors because of the way they see themselves and the situation—they behave in ways that make sense to them based on their perceptions. They, in fact, see no other alternative. A serious flaw in this is its tendency to reject our capacity to evaluate situations, make responsible choices, determine outcomes, and eventually change the ways we see ourselves and the conditions around us.

An extremely narrow yet popular belief of psychic vampirism explains the phenomenon as basically an issue of good versus evil. It says psychic vampirism is more than an energy phenomenon—it is an encounter between the vampire bent on evil and the unsuspecting, innocent victim. Driven by dark, malicious forces, the psychic vampire seeks not only energy but domination and, in some instances, even destruction of the unsuspecting victim. Combating vampirism focuses on repulsing and defeating the vampire, who is then forced to find an unwitting victim elsewhere, a strategy that unfortunately perpetuates the vampire cycle. By focusing on morality issues only, this simplistic belief overlooks the developmental nature and complex functions of the human energy system. For the victim, it prescribes procedures that hold little relevance for long-term growth and personal empowerment.

By looking at psychic vampires as either agents of evil or else hopeless victims of some negative force, it offers little hope for them, many of whom struggle in desperation to overcome the deep-seated conflicts that gave rise to psychic vampirism in the first place. It fails to recognize that psychic vampirism, like other human traits, exists on a continuum. Our studies found, in fact, that the potential for psychic vampirism exists to some extent in everyone, depending on such influences as past experiences and developmental history. As we will discover in a later chapter, most of us possess at least some of the motives and behavioral traits associated with this phenomenon.

The Psychic Empowerment Perspective

In contrast to the above positions, the *psychic empowerment perspective* is a hopeful, positive approach that recognizes the incomparable worth of each human being as a life-force entity with limitless possibilities for growth, change, and personal fulfillment. It acknowledges the mental, physical, and spiritual components of our makeup while emphasizing the interactive nature of each component. The primary focus of this view is on responsible choice and decisive action. We are not hopelessly programmed biological or social machines, but rather evolving beings endowed with the powers of self-determination.

The psychic empowerment perspective views psychic vampirism as developmental in nature. As already noted, almost everyone possesses certain characteristics associated with psychic vampirism. Examples are insecurity, conflict, frustration, and feelings of inferiority, all of which exist on a continuum that ranges from very mild to markedly severe. At lower levels, these traits are normal in that they do not interfere with our personal growth or well-being. But at higher level, they can block our progress, consume our energies, and predispose us to psychic vampirism.

As applied to psychic vampirism, the psychic empowerment perspective is a hopeful view that rejects all alibis and excuses. The potential for greatness exists in everyone. It is up to each of us to discover new ways of empowering our lives, and once empowered, to promote the empowerment of others. Even psychic vampires can master their self-destructive drives by coming to terms with themselves and taking responsibility for their actions. As we will later discover, workable strategies are now available, not only to protect the potential host victim, but to liberate the psychic vampire as well.

From the psychic empowerment perspective, it is the search for meaning that differentiates human beings from all other creation. Only through self-awareness and insight can we develop our highest potentials and take command of the forces that affect our lives. Self-knowledge alone is enriching and empowering. Almost without exception, psychic vampires have but limited understanding of themselves and the meaning of their existence.

According to the psychic empowerment perspective, psychic vampirism is more than an energy phenomenon. It is a developmental dilemma of cosmic proportions. It is largely a product of cosmic insensitivity, imbalance, and separation. Cosmically impoverished, psychic vampires are alienated from the two major dimensions of life-force energy—*the one within the self and the other in the higher cosmos.* With their inner resources exhausted and their personal growth virtually sidetracked, they become enfeebled and, in some instances, desperate in their search for a substitute source of energy.

The step-by-step strategies presented throughout this book embrace the psychic empowerment perspective. They focus on the critical importance of balance within the self and attunement to the highest cosmic sources of energy and power. They recognize the dignity and worth of all human beings. They acknowledge the potential for new insight, growth, and greatness in everyone. They emphasize our limitless capacity to overcome growth barriers and unleash new growth energies. They challenge us to conquer adversity and achieve higher levels of enlightenment. Because of their sweeping nature, they are relevant to almost any personal goal. Hopefully, they will inspire us to enthusiastically embrace change within, while at the same time, reaching beyond ourselves and finding new ways of making the world a better place for all.

Psychic Vampirism Today

Historically, our concept of psychic vampirism has been limited, and the extent of psychic vampirism throughout the world has been grossly underestimated. We now know that psychic vampirism is not only widespread; it also exists in many forms, some of which we have already mentioned in passing. Taken together, contemporary psychic vampirism can be grouped into three major categories:

1. **One-on-one Psychic Vampirism.** This category includes any form of psychic vampirism between two persons, the one being the psychic vampire and the other the host victim. In the typical one-on-one vampire encounter, the psychic vampire taps into the energy system of the host victim for the express purpose of extracting energy. The vampire episode can be consensual or nonconsensual as well as deliberate or

spontaneous. Whatever the nature of the vampire encounter, the results are the same—an instant but transient surge of energy for the vampire, and a critical loss of energy for the vampirized victim. Unfortunately, the psychic vampire's energy needs are satisfied only temporarily, thus necessitating repeated attacks. For the host victim of recurrent attacks, the long-term consequences can be extremely harmful.

2. **Group Psychic Vampirism.** This category, which we could call collective vampirism, includes any form of vampirism that involves groups, organizations, or institutions. In its most insidious and destructive form, it can involve the organized vampire efforts of large numbers of persons. Power, wealth, and control are among the major goals of group vampirism. Its wide-ranging symptoms can include criminal activity, environmental pollution, irresponsible exploitation of the earth's natural resources, and flagrant abuse of human rights. When sufficiently widespread and culturally ingrained, group psychic vampirism can be so powerful that it affects global conditions with consequences that can span centuries.

3. **Parasitic Vampirism.** In sharp contrast to other forms of psychic vampirism, parasitic vampirism is an internal form of psychic vampirism turned against the self. Tragically, parasitic vampires are twice the victim—they are both vampire and host victim. They are driven by self-destructive mechanisms that are like bloodsucking vampires with a demonic appetite—the more they devour, the more they demand. The effects of parasitic vampirism are relentlessly self-constricting and self-disempowering. By attacking from the inside, parasitic vampirism drains its host of essential energy and weakens the ability to cope, even with minor stress. In the long run, parasitic vampirism grinds down the self's energy system and seriously impairs its capacity to generate new energy. Almost invariably, parasitic vampirism generates an inner state of vulnerability that is often the forerunner to other forms of psychic vampirism.

In later chapters, we will further explore each of these major categories of psychic vampirism. Always, our emphasis is on the abundant resources available to us, both within and outside ourselves. Throughout this book, the importance of new insight and responsible action is our constant focus.

For the most part, psychic vampirism is characterized by certain common features:

Psychic vampirism demands a designated victim. The end results are always detrimental for both vampire and host victim.

Psychic vampires have no special powers. They, in fact, operate from a position of weakness rather than strength. Typically underdeveloped or impaired in their ability to generate self-sustaining energy, they turn in desperation to other strategies in their efforts to meet their energy needs.

Psychic vampires are not hopeless creatures of evil. Like everyone, they are persons of significance and inherent worth. Unfortunately their growth is thwarted and their internal energy system is to some extent dysfunctional.

Psychic vampirism is a cultural universal—it exists in one form or another around the world. Even the most highly advanced cultures are vulnerable to the multiple forms of psychic vampirism.

A wide range of conditions can provide fertile breeding grounds for psychic vampirism. Examples are personal crises, thwarted growth, unresolved conflict, and severe stress as well as certain cultural conditions such as social unrest and class resentments.

Psychic vampirism occurs in varying degrees of intensity. It often begins as a mild impulse, then progressively increases to become a dominant force in the life of the psychic vampire.

The long-term consequences of psychic vampirism are enormously detrimental. For the vampire, they can include a rapid depletion of inner resources, and eventually, a total blockage of the growth process. For the victim, they can include a host of mental and physical symptoms.

The psychic vampire attack can be either deliberate or sponta-neous. Although psychic vampire episodes are often intentionally initiated by the vampire, they can be spontaneous and, in some instances, unconscious. Strange as it may seem, psychic vampirism can become a consensual component in certain social relationships, a phenomenon we will later discuss.

Aside from their needs for energy, psychic vampires are often driven by other motives. A man or woman who exploits or ruins a lover out of revenge, for instance, can be seen as a psychic vampire. Corporations that recklessly pollute the environment for profit can be seen as predator organizations.

Empowerment strategies are now available to counteract psychic vampirism. Included are procedures designed (1) to protect the potential victim against a psychic vampire attack, (2) to end the vampire attack once it is in progress, (3) to liberate the active psychic vampire and banish the vampire drive, and finally, 4) to prevent the development of psychic vampirism by promoting a healthy, fully functional energy system within the self.

At my lectures and seminars, the mere mention of psychic vampirism usually generates spirited discussion. Almost everyone relates to the concept, and reports of personal encounters with psychic vampires are common. Here are some of the questions often raised by my audiences concerning psychic vampirism.

1. How do psychic vampires differ from folklore or fictional vampires?

In contrast to folklore and fictional vampirism, psychic vampires feed on energy rather than blood, and they possess no supernatural powers. Deficient in energy, and with their energy system usually impaired, they seek other energy options. Contrary to prevailing stereotypes, typical psychic vampires are not agents of evil bent on the destruction of their victims. Although certain fringe "vampire groups" are known to practice various folklore vampire rituals, they have demonstrated none of the supernatural powers attributed to folklore vampires.

2. How prevalent is psychic vampirism?

Though the exact extent of psychic vampirism is unknown, it is believed to be widespread in its various forms throughout the world.

3. What causes psychic vampirism?

Although the causes vary (depending on the form of psychic vampirism), they usually include a combination of developmental and situational factors. For one-on-one as well as parasitic vampirism, early childhood experiences, including parent-child relationships, are especially critical. Children who are either pampered or who have a cold, distant relationship with either parent seem to be particularly prone to psychic vampirism. Also, certain personality characteristics such as identity conflict, a poor self-image, and deep-seated insecurity and inferiority are common among psychic vampires of both sexes. Psychic vampirism can be precipitated by situational factors such as severely traumatic events, occupational problems, and family crises, to mention only a few of the possibilities. On a larger scale, group psychic vampirism is often associated with corrupt motives and sweeping misuse of power and influence.

4. Is psychic vampirism a recent phenomenon?

Evidence suggests that psychic vampirism long predated folklore and fictional versions of vampirism. The history of civilization is replete with instances of psychic vampirism in its various forms.

5. Are there female as well as male vampires?

Psychic vampires, like their folklore counterparts, can be either male or female. The exact gender ratio is at present unknown.

6. How dangerous is a single psychic vampire attack?

The typical psychic vampire episode is an energy phenomenon in which the vampire is infused with a fresh supply of energy at the expense of the victim donor. While the loss of energy for the donor can be minimal or barely noticeable, even a single vampire attack can have serious consequences, depending on the conditions of the attack as well as the mental and physical states of the host victim. A psychic vampire attack can be especially dangerous in situations requiring alertness and concentration. Imagine, for instance, the possible consequences of a vampire attack against a surgeon during surgery, a soldier in combat, the pilot of a plane, a high-rise construction worker, a driver in heavy traffic, or a world leader during critical negotiations.

7. What are the effects of repeated psychic vampire attacks on the victim?

For the victim of recurrent psychic vampire attacks, the typical effects are a significant loss of energy and, in the long run, damage to the internal energy system itself. Other common effects are chronic fatigue, difficult concentrating, sleep disturbances, irritability, lowered tolerance for frustration, depressed mood, excessive anxiety, sexual indifference, and impaired memory. Extreme, long-term exposure to psychic vampirism can result in biological wear-and-tear accompanied by an array of physical symptoms, including a compromised immune system and even life-threatening illness. There is some evidence to suggest that certain chronic respiratory problems and gastrointestinal disturbances are associated with recurrent psychic vampire attacks.

8. What are the long-term effects of psychic vampirism on the vampire?

Over time, the psychic vampire drive can become so powerful that it dominates the person's life. Eventually, virtually every aspect of the vampire's life centers around meeting critical energy needs. Unfortunately, as the vampire drive becomes stronger, the vampire's inner energy mechanisms slowly deteriorate like muscles that are never used. The vampire's inner energy system can become so fragile that it is finally short-circuited and rendered totally nonfunctional. Like an essential body organ that no longer functions, the incapacitated energy system requires external life-support. In the case of psychic vampirism, that life support is the energy system of a host victim.

9. What is the relationship, if any, between psychic vampirism and violence?

Failure of the psychic vampire to meet personal energy demands can cause frustration, panic, anger, and even violence. Although violent behavior is not typically representative of psychic vampirism, our case studies of violent offenders suggested an interesting link between aggressive behavior and full-blown psychic vampirism. Frustrated in their efforts to satisfy their energy needs, psychic vampires may turn to dangerous acting-out. Unfortunately, the risk of violence seems to increase in long-term psychic vampire situations, including consensual vampire relationships in which a particular partner decides to terminate the relationship.

10. Can psychic vampires strike from a distance?

Vampire attacks can occur during physical contact—such as a handshake or touch on the shoulder—or they can occur at distances of up to many miles. Vampire assaults involving great distances, however, are associated only with advanced psychic vampirism. They usually occur in the context of an ongoing association or relationship, though not necessarily of the romantic kind. Psychic vampire attacks can also occur during astral travel, a phenomenon we will discuss in a later chapter. There is sketchy evidence to suggest that psychic vampirism can involve discarnate beings, a possibility we will also explore later.

11. What are the attack strategies used by psychic vampires?

The attack strategies used by psychic vampires vary, depending on the type of vampirism and the surrounding conditions. The deliberate vampire attack typically consists of (1) a focused mental state in which the host victim is the object of attention, (2) a strong intent to tap the energy system of the victim, and (3) forcefully taking energy from the victim. Interviews with experienced psychic vampires found that imagery of an energy channel connecting them to their host victim throughout the attack is common. In the spontaneous attack, the strategies are similar but effortless and at times, unconscious.

Often underlying the psychic vampire attack are certain hidden motives, such as domination, punishment, and control. The energizing effects of subduing others and forcefully taking energy from them are often secondary to the rewards of the conquest itself.

12. Is there any hope for the psychic vampire?

Fortunately, advanced strategies as already noted are now available, not only to protect and empower the potential victim, but also to liberate the psychic vampire. For the vampire, the recovery process must include a recognition of the disempowering nature of psychic vampirism on both vampire and victim, a firm resolve to develop a more functional internal energy system, and, finally, mastery of relevant recovery strategies.

Unfortunately, the popular notions of evil associated with psychic vampirism contribute to the vampire's tendency toward self-rejection and complicates any recovery effort. At the same time, attributing evil to psychic vampirism handicaps the potential victim's efforts to acquire effective vampire protection and coping skills. Also, the "vampire" label itself can encourage rejection of the psychic vampire who is too often seen as a depraved, deviant creature to be avoided at all costs. Such exaggerated stereotyping can actually increase our vulnerability to psychic vampirism. It is possible to become so vampire phobic in our perception of psychic vampirism as an evil threat that fear alone consumes enormous amounts of our energy, thus actually exhausting our defense and coping resources. The energy wasted on false perceptions and exaggerated fear could be put to much better use, such as energizing our personal development and perhaps helping others.

13. What is the best defense against psychic vampirism?

The best defense against psychic vampirism is a strong internal energy system, a state of inner balance and attunement, and mastery of relevant psychic empowerment strategies. In the following chapters, we will present highly detailed ways to prevent a psychic vampire attack or to promptly repel it once it is underway. The constant thrust of this book is toward promoting awareness of psychic vampirism in its variety of forms while providing workable prevention and intervention strategies that can be used by everyone.

Summary

Psychic vampirism is, without doubt, one of the most intriguing phenomena involving human behavior. It is also one of the most complex. It's easy to mistake psychic vampirism as either fictional or simply more juicy sensationalism, but a closer look reveals a serious reality so common that almost everyone has had some experience with it, and for some, it is a recurring dilemma.

Although the expression "psychic vampirism" as typically applied denotes a social phenomenon in which the vampire invades the energy system of another person for the express purpose of extracting energy, it can range from self-contained parasitic vampirism, in which the victim is oneself, to global vampirism involving social injustices on a massive scale. In whatever its form, psychic vampirism can have potentially devastating consequences.

While contemporary psychic vampirism is usually seen as the modern counterpart of ancient vampire folklore, there is evidence indicating that psychic vampirism predated folklore and may have, in fact, provided the seminal inspiration for its fictional, bloodsucking counterpart. Whatever the sequence of events, vampires of both the fictional and psychic kind share certain common characteristics. Both are stalled in their personal growth, both are devoid of personal fulfillment, and both require victims from whom they extract a critical life-sustaining resource.

Psychic vampirism is developmental in nature. The same conditions that promote healthy mental and physical growth—a sense of personal worth, an optimistic outlook, an inner set of guiding values, and commitment to important life goals—likewise promote a strong internal energy system. An absence of these essentials interrupts our growth and increases our vulnerability to psychic vampirism.

Understanding psychic vampirism and mastering the skills required to counteract it are critical to our personal growth and well being. Whether in our personal lives or in the work setting, it is important that we understand the forces that influence our success and the quality of our lives. A working knowledge of psychic vampirism enables us to acquire essential empowerment skills, while at the same time, helping us to better understand ourselves and our interactions with others.

TWO

The Energies of Life

PSYCHIC VAMPIRISM IS fundamentally an energy phenomenon. Understanding psychic vampirism, and more importantly, mastering the empowerment strategies related to it, require a closer look at not one but two critical energy systems—the one within ourselves and the other in the higher cosmos. Together, these two important systems constantly interact to energize our existence as a life-force entity.

The forms and manifestations of energy are endless. The universe itself is built on energy. All that exists—both seen and unseen, tangible and intangible—is an expression of energy. Whether we scan the heavens with the naked eye, or survey the earth's natural wonders around us, we see energy. Whether we probe deep space through a telescope or observe a unicellular organism through a microscope, we see energy. Each work of nature whispers in our ear, *I am energy.* At a deeply personal level, when we look within ourselves, we see energy. Thinking, feeling, acting, and simply being—all are manifestations of energy. The simple assertion, *I am energy,* is among the most elemental and yet profound observations we can make about ourselves and the nature of our existence in the universe.

Energy as a fundamental life force not only sustains life, it gave rise to life in the beginning. As already noted, there are two major systems of life-force energy: the *internal energy system,* which exists within ourselves, and the *cosmic energy system,* which exists throughout the known universe and beyond. Designed to work together, these life-force energy systems provide the propelling force that energizes our total being—mentally, physically, and spiritually. Among the major purposes of our existence are: first, to develop our potential for a powerful internal energy system; and second, to bring that inner system into balance and attunement with the higher cosmic system, the energizing origin of our existence. Only through achieving these goals can we find meaning to our lives and eventually reach our highest destiny. In the following discussion, we will examine these two energy systems and explore their relevance to psychic vampirism.

The Internal Energy System

A strong internal energy system has two important functions related to psychic vampirism: first, it ensures an abundant supply of essential energy within the self, thus eliminating any need for psychic vampire tactics in meeting our personal energy needs; and second, it repels any external threat of a psychic vampire attack on our energy system.

The self's internal energy system, like other aspects of our being, consists of three essential interactive components—mental, physical, and spiritual. Although the mental and physical aspects of our makeup have long been accepted by conventional thinking as critical to our personal well-being, only recently has mainstream science begun to recognize the spiritual component and its importance in daily life. Reflecting this trend is the American Psychological Association's recent listing of recommended readings for psychologists, which included for the first time books designed to introduce spirituality into the professional practice of psychology. Of particular interest is a recommended book on "theistic spirituality," which holds that human beings have an eternal spirit and that God communicates with them through spiritual channels.

Joining psychology in demonstrating a greater awareness and appreciation of the spiritual nature of our makeup is modern medicine. The healing value of faith, prayer, and meditation is now recognized in many medical settings. In my clinical practice, I routinely use spiritual strategies because of their singular therapeutic benefits. In future medicine, promoting healing, balance, and well-being through spiritual channels will undoubtedly increase. As we will later see, a major characteristic found among psychic vampires is the absence of inner balance and well-being. By the same token, a state of inner balance and well-being is one of our best defenses against psychic vampirism.

In finally acknowledging the importance of spirituality, modern health sciences have edged closer to recognizing a higher cosmic energy system as the life-force counterpart of the self's internal energy system. Consistent with that recognition is an emerging acceptance of our cosmic origin. From there, it requires no quantum leap to conclude with reasonable certainty the indestructible nature of our existence as a life-force entity.

Every aspect of our being is energized and sustained by the constant flow of life-force energy. When we are enriched with life-force energy, our mental, physical, and spiritual functions flourish. But when we are deficient in essential life-force energy, they falter. Psychic vampirism, in whatever its form, taps into our energy resources and consumes vital life-force energy. In the worst scenario, the internal energy system can malfunction and critical coping resources can become virtually exhausted. Eventually, the growth process can become totally arrested, particularly in instances of severe and repeated vampire attacks. It becomes plausible then that mastery of effective vampire protection strategies is indeed critical to our total growth and evolvement as human beings.

The flow of life-force energy within the self has a definite direction. By exercising its energizing powers, the internal energy system not only maintains itself, it opens new growth channels and generates new growth energy. Failing to exercise its energizing potentials, or even worse, expressing itself negatively through self-destructive channels, leads to energy loss, growth blockage, and, in the long term, damage to the system itself. It would follow that an empowered internal energy system is not only critical to our personal growth, it is our first line of defense against psychic vampirism.

Fortunately, we can take command of the internal energy system by activating and directing its functions. This can be done in somewhat the same way that an electrical control panel directs the flow of electrical energy. A powerful *energy control panel,* with switches and lines, exists within each of us just waiting to be used. We can close down old, inefficient energy channels and open up new, more efficient channels. We can activate totally new mental channels to enrich intellectual processes or stimulate totally new mental functions, such as accelerating learning, improving memory, and increasing creativity, to mention only a few of the possibilities. By interacting with the energy control panel within, we can close down channels that energize destructive anxieties, depression, inferiority, and inner conflicts—all of which increase our vulnerability to psychic vampirism in its multiple forms. We can open up new physical channels to energize biological organs and systems. We can fortify the body's immune system, accelerate healing, and even slow the aging process. We can shut down energy channels that enfeeble the physical body and render it vulnerable to psychic vampirism. By taking charge of the control panel within, we can open spiritual channels that connect us to the highest cosmic source of pure energy. We can rediscover our cosmic roots and regain our oneness with the universe. We can unleash an unlimited flow of spiritual renewal. Infused with new spiritual energy, we can emerge enlightened, emboldened, enriched, and fully empowered.

In addition to its major mental, physical, and spiritual components, the internal energy system has a built-in *energy defense potential* with the capacity to repel any invading energy force, including psychic vampirism. That capacity functions best when our internal energy channels are open and functional. But even then, our deliberate intervention is often required to activate the energy system's defense potential.

Fortunately, strategies are now available to empower the internal energy system and activate each of its specific functions. Aside from opening up new energy channels and closing down inefficient ones, we can:

- Repair any damage to the internal energy system and reinforce its multiple functions.
- Integrate the mental, physical, and spiritual sources of energy within the self.
- Fortify the energy system's defense and coping potentials.
- Attune and balance the self's energy system to the highest cosmic source of unlimited energy.

We will later present step-by-step procedures designed to achieve each of these empowerment goals.

Because the human energy system is mental, physical, and spiritual, psychic vampirism is more than simply a physical phenomenon. It is also mental and spiritual. Hence to be effective, psychic vampire defense and coping strategies must address each of these components and their related functions. For instance, mental components can include strategies that activate the mind's power to confront and subdue the onslaught of psychic vampirism. Physical components can include strategies that promote a balanced physical state that spontaneously repels psychic vampirism. Finally, spiritual components can include strategies that connect us to the higher cosmos and create a protective shield that envelopes us totally. Together, these mental, physical, and spiritual components, when appropriately incorporated into step-by-step procedures, will interact to generate abundant energy and an empowered energy system that simply cannot fail.

Fortunately, the same procedures that empower the energy system invariably enrich every aspect of our lives. Through them, we discover new growth resources; we become empowered to achieve important life goals; we learn to deal more effectively with stress; and perhaps most importantly, we become acutely aware of our connection to the highest cosmic sources of power and enlightenment. Success and personal fulfillment become actual realities rather than distant, nebulous possibilities.

The Outer Cosmic Energy System

The outer cosmic energy system, like the energy system within ourselves, is an interactive system. It is the source of life-force energy in its purest form. Once created, cosmic life-force energy cannot be destroyed. It constantly interacts with our own internal energy system to sustain it and ensure our survival as a perpetual life-force entity. To put it simply, the cosmic energy system is our ever-present partner in the higher cosmos. Without it, we would not exist.

As energized beings whose origin is cosmic, we are each endowed with a unique cosmic makeup, which we call our *cosmic genotype.* Our cosmic genotype is the spiritual counterpart of our *biological genotype,* or genetic makeup. Put in analogy form, our cosmic genotype is to the spirit as our biological genotype is to the body. While the makeup of our physical body varies from life to life, the makeup of our cosmic body remains unchanged, thereby ensuring our individuality and the uniqueness of our cosmic identity. Although we may require many different lifetimes with many different interactive roles in many different cultures to achieve our highest growth potentials, each life retains its basic, indestructible cosmic design. Within that unique sameness which provides continuity from life to life, each lifetime offers a new biological genotype with new resources and opportunities for our personal evolvement.

Since we are all different in our cosmic identity and design (no two souls are exactly alike), we can each contribute to the world in ways different from those of any other human being. Today, perhaps more than ever before, it is critical that we recognize the importance of diversity, both within ourselves and throughout the globe. In recent years, enlightened leaders around the world have cried out for diversity. They figured out early on that the solution to some of our most pressing global problems—war, hunger, disease, environmental pollution, and so forth—requires the skills and cooperation of the world's diverse cultures. Like globally oriented leaders who were ahead of their times, many modern business and industrial organizations now actively promote diversity. Employees representing a variety of backgrounds, specializations, and orientations bring with them invaluable resources that enrich the organization and promote global progress, which is particularly critical to international firms.

While diversity and individual uniqueness are critical to global progress, our similarities as human beings are likewise important. Whatever our backgrounds and individual differences, we are more alike than different. By recognizing our similarities, we understand each other better, and we work together more harmoniously in achieving our common goals. Appreciating our similarities while at the same time valuing our individual differences is the hallmark of cultural progress and productive social interaction. As we will later discover, psychic vampires are often rigid in their perceptions of others and intolerant of values and orientations that differ even moderately from their own.

As a unique life-force entity, our personal growth exists on an endless cosmic continuum that reaches into our most distant past and stretches to infinity. In the beginning, we were not created to age and die, but to live and grow. All the accumulated experiences of our past lives, along with our between-life experiences, are a part of our cosmic life span, which is eternal. Even our existence before our first incarnation, which we commonly call our *pre-incarnate life,* remains an integral component of our total being.

Although many of our past experiences are stored in the subconscious and thus unknown to conscious awareness, they nevertheless remain an integral part of our being. Because our cosmic identity was fixed at the very beginning of our existence, we are at any moment in time the totality of our experiences—nothing is ever permanently lost. A major task in each lifetime is not only to discovery new knowledge, but to retrieve the knowledge buried deeply in the subconscious. Given knowledge of our past-life experiences, we can identify and resolve the subconscious conflicts of past-life origin that continue to influence our life, and in many instances impede our growth. We can uncover important subconscious resources and activate dormant potentials required to solve present-life problems. The resultant possibilities for enlightenment and new growth are simply unlimited. In psychic vampirism, the task of rediscovering the self is almost always interrupted by either resistance or simply a lack of motivation.

The inner and outer energy systems underlying our existence can be seen as interacting fountains of limitless growth potential. While their functions differ, both fountains are essential sources of sustaining energy. The higher cosmic fountain is, however, preeminent—its energizing and sustaining power is infinite. Even when biological systems fail and death finally leans against the door, the outer cosmic fountain energizes our safe transition to the other side. It ensures our permanent survival as a conscious, life-force entity. Upon our transition to the other side, it instantly restores us to the highest peaks of all our past development, and from there, it energizes our future growth. We are at once restored, rejuvenated, and renewed in that higher dimension where all the abundant resources we need for our continued growth are always present.

Although the cosmic fountain of energy is always available to us, it is up to each us to responsibly use it. By accessing that fountain and tapping its powerful energy, we can instantly add meaning and value to our lives. Energized by the cosmic fountain of life, we can overcome adversity and find new hope and peace. By accessing that fountain, we can become energized to determine our own destiny and achieve our highest goals. Imbued with abundant cosmic energy, we can accelerate our growth and experience a deeper meaning to our existence. In a word, we can become *empowered*. What better defense against psychic vampirism than to be energized by the highest fountain of power in the cosmos!

By interacting with the cosmic energy system, we can fortify our inner system and maximize its capacity to generate powerful energy. As a result, we can become attuned and balanced, both within ourselves and with the cosmos. Such a cosmic connection invariably gives rise to a more positive self-identity, a sense of personal worth, and feelings of security and well-being, all of which are themselves energizing. Imbued and revitalized with positive energy, we function with independence and self-reliance, characteristics which are either weak or totally absent in the psychic vampire.

A major characteristic of the cosmic energy system is its multiple planes of energy, each with its own particular characteristics and functions. Once linked to the cosmic system of energy, we can identify those planes that are relevant to our present goals, and then draw from their specialized resources. We will later explore a variety of cosmic energy planes and develop advanced strategies that enable us to access their powers.

Admittedly, neither realizing our highest growth potentials nor achieving our highest life goals is always easy. At one time or another, we all encounter conditions that slow our progress and challenge our resolve. Certain adverse life situations can be particularly distressful. Examples are life-threatening illness, severe financial reversals, and threats to our personal security and well-being, all of which can impair important areas of our functioning. Fortunately, adversity in the long haul is no match for the cosmically empowered self. Even the most extreme adversity cannot destroy the inner potential for greatness. When attuned, balanced, and energized, we can learn from adversity and overcome the repelling forces that, at first, seemed beyond our control and impossible to bear. Encountering the adversities of life and successfully overcoming them are among our most difficult yet valuable challenges.

The Handclasp of Power

Fortunately, the energy system within each of us is always receptive to our empowerment efforts. We can deliberately generate a powerful inner state that protects the system and maximizes its energizing potentials. We can repair damage to the system, revitalize ineffective mechanisms, and open up totally new energy pathways. We can attune and balance the system to the highest cosmic source of pure energy. We can empower the system to resist the onslaught of any negative force, including psychic vampirism. The Handclasp of Power is designed to achieve each of these important goals.

This powerful strategy, which requires only a few minutes, is one of our best defenses against psychic vampirism.

Step 1. **Body Scan.** Settle back and while breathing slowly and rhythmically, mentally scan your body from your head downward, briefly pausing at areas of tension. Visualize the tension as a shadowy mist and your conscious presence a luminous glow. Let the glow of consciousness repel the shadowy mist and replace it with bright, new, radiant energy. Take plenty of time for the luminous glow of your conscious presence to fully permeate your physical body.

Step 2. **Focusing.** Focus your conscious awareness on your solar plexus, and think of that region as your energy control center. Visualize your conscious presence at that center as a bright, supercharged force that activates and fortifies your total energy system.

Step 3. **Self-infusion.** As you remain consciously centered, visualize energy pathways extending outward from your inner control center. You can now identify blocked pathways and open them up to unleash a totally new flow of life-force energy. You can now replace old, nonfunctional pathways with shining, new energy channels. Let the supercharging flow of powerful energy illuminate your total being, inside and out.

Step 4. **Cosmic Infusion.** Turn your hands upward as you sense radiant beams of pure cosmic energy entering your palms and then spreading inward to bathe and energize every part of your being. Sense vibrant cosmic energy flowing throughout your energy system, saturating it totally with bright cosmic energy.

Step 5. Attunement and Balance. Clasp your hands as a symbol of your oneness with the cosmos. Affirm: *I am now totally balanced and attuned to the higher cosmos.* You can use the handclasp at will as a cue to activate the empowering effects of the full procedure.

With practice, this procedure becomes increasingly effective in energizing, balancing, and attuning the energy system. This procedure also promotes alertness and clear thinking while protecting against the invasion of negative forces in any form. It is especially useful when practiced prior to important meetings, particularly when they involve challenging negotiations and problem-solving. Having practiced the full procedure, you can use the inconspicuous handclasp cue almost anytime. It can be used during conferences and public presentations to instantly increase your effectiveness and sense of command over the situation at hand. Many speakers and performers use the cue routinely both before and during public appearances.

The Handclasp of Power is a basic, all-purpose strategy that generates a powerful, energized state of growth readiness throughout the self. When practiced regularly, it can increase the effectiveness of each of the empowerment procedures that follows throughout this book.

Summary

Two major systems of energy constantly interact to sustain our existence and energize our growth. The unfailing energy system in the higher cosmos supports our existence and ensures our survival as a conscious life-force entity from life to life and beyond. Its counterpart, the energy system within each of us, is designed to generate an abundant inner flow of mental, physical, and spiritual energy. It is our ever-present link to the higher cosmos.

Only when we balance and attune our internal energy system to the highest cosmic source of energy can we achieve our ultimate destiny for growth and greatness. Psychic vampirism in its many forms is a threat to our personal actualization and well-being. Fortunately, procedures are now available to repel psychic vampirism, fortify our internal energy system, and finally bring us into complete oneness with the cosmic source of our existence.

THREE

One-on-One
Psychic Vampirism

ONE-ON-ONE psychic vampirism is a form of social vampirism in which one person, typically called the *psychic vampire*, extracts energy from another person, typically called the *host victim*. The results are a temporary surge of new energy for the psychic vampire and an immediate loss of energy for the unfortunate host victim.

As with other types of psychic vampirism, one-on-one psychic vampirism seems to be very widespread. If you take a moment to reflect, you may recall having experienced this unpleasant phenomenon which drained you of energy and left you both mentally and physically fatigued. You may have, in fact, sensed the violation of your personal space and the actual siphoning of energy from your body as the vampire encounter progressed. Once aware of these effects, you may have sought polite ways to end the intrusion. Even if you did not attribute the energy loss and resultant fatigue to psychic vampirism, the experience may have been so intensely exhaustive that you found yourself more guarded in similar future situations, or you may have avoided them altogether. It is interesting to note that some of the terms we use to describe such unpleasant social encounters clearly imply psychic vampirism—"a pain in the neck," "under my skin," and "a draining experience" are examples.

Fortunately for most of us, our social interactions are usually energizing as well as rewarding in other ways. And while many of our interactions involve a two-way exchange of energy, they do not necessarily suggest one-on-one vampirism at work, even when the benefits of the interaction are not equal. We have probably all participated in social interactions that were somewhat one-sided. In fact, deliberately managing or manipulating social interactions to gain a particular goal or advantage is generally tolerated in our culture; and in many situations it is a social expectation. Familiar examples are the bombardment of persuasive communications seen regularly in politics, religion, fundraising, and advertising. Perhaps with some reluctance, we could add to these our own experiences in which we orchestrated situations and interactions that expressly benefited us socially or professionally. But while these examples alone do not indicate psychic vampirism, they do suggest certain inclinations that, if cultivated, could lead to active vampirism. Experienced psychic vampires, in fact, often present a long history of manipulating people and situations to advance their careers or other self-interests, a pattern that became increasingly dominant and eventually led to full-fledged psychic vampirism.

In an effort to determine the frequency of vampire-like social interactions, students enrolled in a social psychology course at Athens State College (now University) conducted a study in which they interviewed 100 shoppers at a mall during a busy holiday season. To control bias and promote validity, the Interaction Interview Guide used for the study intentionally omitted such potentially loaded terms as "psychic vampire" and "psychic vampirism." Here is the twelve-item interview guide with the percentage of responses obtained for each item (see following page).

A large majority of respondents in this survey viewed themselves as socially outgoing (82 percent). A slightly larger number viewed their social interactions as typically satisfying or rewarding (84 percent), although many of them qualified their responses with such

Interaction Interview Guide

I am a student enrolled in a social psychology course at Athens State College. In partial fulfillment of course requirements, I am conducting a survey concerning social interaction. Would you take just a moment to answer a few question about your own social interactions?

1. Do you think of yourself as a socially outgoing person? 82% Yes; 5% No; 13% Undecided.

2. As a rule, are your interactions with other persons usually satisfying? 84% Yes; 12% No; 4% Undecided.

3. Do you find special satisfaction through your interactions with a particular individual or individuals? 80% Yes; 20% No; 0% Undecided.

4. Do you sometimes feel energized or full of energy following your interactions with a certain person or persons? 92% Yes; 6% No; 2% Undecided.

5. Do you sometimes feel fatigued or low of energy following your interactions with a certain person or persons? 97% Yes; 2% No; 1% Undecided.

6. In your opinion, do certain persons tend to contribute or "give off" energy to other persons through their interactions with them. 79% Yes; 10% No; 11% Undecided.

7. In your opinion, do certain persons tend to drain energy from other persons through their interactions with them? 85% Yes; 2% No; 13% Undecided.

8. Do you sometimes energize others by contributing energy to them during your interactions with them? 40% Yes; 21% No; 39% Undecided.

9. Are you sometimes energized by receiving energy from others during your interactions with them? 80% Yes; 11% No; 9% Undecided.

10. Do you interact regularly with someone who drains energy from you? 24% Yes; 42% No; 34% Undecided.

11. Do you sometimes avoid interacting with certain persons because they seem to drain you of energy? 88% Yes; 5% No; 7% Undecided.

12. Do you interact regularly with someone who energizes you by contributing energy to you? 10% Yes; 88% No; 2% Undecided.

Thank you for your participation in this survey.

expressions as "More or less" or "I think so." A very high percent of the survey respondents (97 percent) reported past social interactions that left them fatigued or low of energy. Eighty-five percent of the respondents believed that certain individuals tend to drain energy from others through their interactions with them. A slightly lower percent (79 percent) believed that certain individuals tend to contribute energy to others. A large number of our respondents (88 percent) reported that they sometimes avoided interacting with certain individuals who, they believed, drained energy from them. Only 40 percent of the respondents believed they contributed energy to others during their interactions with them; whereas 80 percent believed they received energy from others during their interactions. Twenty-four percent of the respondents admitted that they interacted regularly with persons who drained them of energy; whereas only 10 percent of the respondents admitted regularly interacting with persons who contributed energy to them.

Taken together, the results of this survey suggest that vampire-like social interactions are common, with almost everyone having experienced some from of energy transaction in which they experienced a depletion of their energy resources. By the same token, almost everyone reports having experienced a new infusion of energy resulting from their social interactions. It is conceivable, of course, that fluctuations in our energy levels could be explained as a self-contained function of the internal energy system rather than the result of psychic vampirism. But while changes in one's inner energy levels can indeed occur independently of psychic vampirism, a vast majority of this study's respondents reported being consciously aware of the actual draining of energy during their interactions with others—a clear suggestion of psychic vampirism at work.

One of the most subtle forms of psychic vampirism seems to occur during social interactions involving interpersonal communication. Whether verbal or nonverbal, the communication process can be seen as an energy interaction with either empowering or disempowering consequences. Typically, positive communications generate empowering interactions. For instance, messages of hope, acceptance, and love are typically empowering to both the sender and receiver. In contrast, negative messages tend to generate disempowering interactions. But even negative messages can be empowering when appropriately managed by the target receiver. For instance, when we ward off incoming messages of bigotry, prejudice, exclusion, and hate, our energy system's resistance functions are fortified and the potentially enfeebling message is neutralized. Furthermore, the sender's energy system, including its negative sending capacity, is denied reinforcement. At a global level, it would follow that only through active resistance on a massive scale can the vampirism of intolerance and injustice be de-energized and finally banished from the globe. Such resistance must, however, include efforts to infuse the globe with the empowering energies of tolerance and justice.

The Mechanics of One-on-One Psychic Vampirism

One-on-one psychic vampirism is driven by an inadequate internal energy system that demands life-force energy from a host victim. Developmental in nature, one-on-one vampirism is often expressed spontaneously in its early stages of development. But in its full-blown form, it usually consists of acquired skills that are deliberately used to replenish the vampire's internal supply of energy. Unfortunately, simply replenishing the deficient energy supply does not fix the faulty energy system itself. Consequently, psychic vampirism becomes a controlling force that compels the vampire to invade the energy systems of selected host victims. Eventually, the vampire drive becomes so compulsive that it seems to take on a life of its own.

Only recently have we begun to figure out the complex mechanics involved in one-on-one vampirism as an energy phenomenon. As noted earlier in this book, energy is more than physical—it is mental and spiritual as well. As a multidimensional life force, it sustains our conscious existence, not only in the physical realm but in afterlife as well. As earlier noted, among the most important challenges we experience in life are: first, to progressively develop a more powerful life-force energy system within ourselves; and second, to keep that system in constant attunement and balance with the higher cosmos. The psychic vampire has failed to some extent on both counts. Driven by a deficient system and either unable or unwilling to correct it, psychic vampires turn to the energy system of others to meet their energy needs. The unfortunate consequences encompass every aspect of the vampire's growth and development. The internal energy system is progressively enfeebled, social interactions are disrupted, and adjustment resources are eventually exhausted.

Our studies of one-on-one psychic vampirism focused first on identifying and measuring the personal characteristics associated with the phenomenon and second on formulating workable, step-by-step empowerment procedures for use not only to empower the victim (or potential victim) of psychic vampirism but also to liberate the psychic vampire from a disempowering lifestyle of psychic vampirism. Multidimensional in design, our research included personal interviews, questionnaires, case studies, psychological testing, electrophotographic recordings (Kirlian photography), and analysis of the human aura which is discussed in the next chapter. In some instances, we used dream analysis and hypnosis, including past-life regression. Our investigative methods consistently avoided such loaded terms as "vampire," "victim," and "vampirism," preferring instead more nonthreatening yet operational terms such as "energy recipient," "energy donor," "energy interaction," "energy deficiency," and "energy-transfer process."

Given the many variations of one-on-one vampirism, along with its developmental nature, identifying the characteristics associated with the phenomenon and accurately measurement them were daunting tasks. Throughout, our approach emphasized psychic vampirism, not as a dark aberration, but as a constellation of characteristics which exist on a continuum of intensity.

Based on the early findings of our studies, we developed two objective tests for measuring tendencies toward one-on-one psychic vampirism. Recently revised, the first test, Interactive Questionnaire IR (see pages 44–45), measures one-on-one vampirism in one's interactions with people in general. Also recently revised, the second test, Interactive Questionnaire IIR, measures one-on-one vampirism in one's relationship with a particular partner. As you will note, neither test mentions vampire or vampirism in a deliberate effort to make the tests as nonthreatening and accurate as possible.

Using the scoring key, the higher the score on this test the greater the tendency toward psychic vampirism in one's interactions with people in general. A score range of 21–25 suggests a severe tendency toward psychic vampirism. A score range of 16–20 suggests a marked tendency toward psychic vampirism. A score range off 11–15 suggests a moderate tendency toward psychic vampirism. A score of 10 or below suggests no significant tendency toward psychic vampirism.

To evaluate the tendency toward psychic vampirism in one's relationship with a particular partner, we formulated the Interactive Questionnaire IIR as follows on pages 46–47. As with Interactive Questionnaire IR, the higher the score on this test the greater the tendency toward psychic vampirism in one's relationship with a particular partner. A score range of 21–25 suggests a severe tendency toward psychic vampirism. A score range of 16–20 suggests a marked tendency toward psychic vampirism. A score range of 11–15 suggests a moderate tendency toward psychic vampirism. A score of 10 or below suggests no significant tendency toward psychic vampirism.

In a study of one-on-one psychic vampirism among undergraduate college students, we administered the Interactive Questionnaire IR to 400 volunteers drawn from the college student population. Over half of them (57 percent) showed a tendency toward psychic vampirism in their relationships with people in general. Of that number, 28 percent showed a moderate tendency toward psychic vampirism, 18 percent showed a marked tendency toward psychic vampirism, and 11 percent showed a severe tendency toward psychic vampirism.

Interaction Questionnaire IR (People in General)

Name: _____ Age: _____ Gender: _____

Directions: This questionnaire is designed to measure certain aspects of your interactions with people in general. Read each statement carefully. If the statement is true as applied to you, circle T. If the statement is false as applied to you, circle F.

T F 1. I often depend on others to do things for me that I could easily do for myself.

T F 2. I believe people are basically honest.

T F 3. I often act on impulse with little thought of the consequences.

T F 4. I often experience a fascinating connection to a total stranger.

T F 5. I am an easygoing person.

T F 6. Most people are out for what they can get in life.

T F 7. I usually find a way of avoiding unpleasant or demanding tasks.

T F 8. Most people make friends because they are useful to them in some way.

T F 9. I often do risky things just for the thrill of it.

T F 10. I am usually determined to get the things I want one way or another.

T F 11. When I am mistreated by someone, I usually find a way of getting even.

T F 12. I tend to thrive on the energies of people around me.

T F 13. Most people are willing to use others to get ahead in life.

T F 14. I am usually forthright in my relationships with others.

T F 15. I am very much concerned about global problems, such as pollution, hunger, and poverty.

T F 16. I find satisfaction in taking advantage of people who leave themselves open to it.

T F 17. I am usually open and honest in my relationships with others.

T F 18. I have learned the hard way not to trust people.

T F 19. I often help others who are less fortunate than myself.

T F 20. At times, I seem to drain energy from persons around me.

T F 21. When I do a favor for someone, I usually expect something in return.

T F 22. I often make friends because they are useful to me in some way.

T F 23. Most people would cheat if they thought they could get away with it.

T F 24. I am basically satisfied with my life.

T F 25. My life is full of meaning.

Scoring Key: Allow one point for each of the following responses: Item 1(T), 2(F), 3(T), 4(T), 5(F), 6(T), 7(T), 8(T), 9(T), 10(T), 11(T), 12(T), 13(T), 14(F), 15(F), 16(T), 17(F), 18(T), 19(F), 20(T), 21(T), 22(T), 23(T), 24(F), 25(F).

Interaction Questionnaire IIR (Partner Relationship)

Name: _____ Age: _____ Gender: _____

Directions: This questionnaire is designed to measure certain aspects of your interactions with your partner. Read each statement carefully. If the statement is true as applied to you, circle T. If the statement is false as applied to you, circle F.

T F   1. My partner is usually alert and full of energy when we are together.

T F   2. I am overly demanding in my relationship with my partner.

T F   3. I receive far more than I give in my relationship with my partner.

T F   4. I make most of the important decisions involving our relationship.

T F   5. In our relationship, my partner is usually submissive to my demands.

T F   6. My partner and I have each grown in our relationship together.

T F   7. My partner is a strong, independent person.

T F   8. When we disagree, my partner usually gives in to my opinions.

T F   9. I am usually forthright in my relationship with my partner.

T F 10. I am quite manipulative in my relationship with my partner.

T F 11. I am usually full of energy, even when I am separated from my partner.

T F 12. I depend on the energy I receive from my relationship with my partner.

T F 13. Should my relationship with my partner end, I would immediately seek another partner.

T F 14. My partner invests a great deal more energy in our relationship than I do.

T F 15. I find satisfaction in having a certain power over my partner.

T F 16. My partner frequently seems hesitant or doubtful regarding our relationship.

T F 17. My partner seldom complains of low energy or fatigue.

T F 18. I seem regularly to drain energy from my partner.

T F 19. I tend to call upon my partner for help, even with things I could easily do for myself.

T F 20. I am the dominant force in my relationship with my partner.

T F 21. My partner usually seems energized by our relationship.

T F 22. My partner and I have a mutually satisfying relationship.

T F 23. I am frequently irritable and aggressive in my interactions with my partner.

T F 24. I often take advantage of my partner in order to achieve my own goals or meet my own needs.

T F 25. My relationship with my partner is one of mutual trust and respect.

Scoring Key: Allow one point for each of the following responses: Item 1(F), 2(T), 3(T), 4(T), 5(T), 6(F), 7(F), 8(T), 9(F), 10(T), 11(F), 12(T), 13(T), 14(T), 15(T), 16(T), 17(F), 18(T), 19(T), 20(T), 21(F), 22(F), 23(T), 24(T), 25(F).

Of the 400 subjects who took the Interactive Questionnaire IR, 183 reported they were in a partner relationship and were administered Interactive Questionnaire IIR to determine the prevalence of psychic vampirism in their relationships with their partners. The results revealed a strong relationship between the two questionnaires. Persons who demonstrated psychic vampire tendencies in their relationships with people-in-general tended to demonstrate similar psychic vampire tendencies in their relationships with their partners.

Follow-up studies of volunteers from the general population revealed a distribution of one-on-one psychic vampire tendencies strongly similar to that of the college student population. Our studies found that both students and nonstudents who took either test invariably showed at least some of the characteristics associated with one-on-one psychic vampirism.

As a word of caution, when using these instruments to test either oneself or others, interpreting the results should recognize the developmental nature of psychic vampirism and the continuum upon which this condition exists. Even a severe tendency toward psychic vampirism, either with people in general or with a particular partner at one time or another, does not conclusively signal the full-blown condition. Only when the tendency is so intense that it interferes with one's own well-being or with the well-being of others should it be considered active psychic vampirism. Almost always, full-blown psychic vampirism is associated with difficulty in such areas as job performance, home life, and, of course, social relationships. Unfortunately, psychic vampirism is all too often unrecognized as a potential source of these difficulties, even when other explanations have been ruled out.

One of the striking findings of our studies was the extensive range of personal characteristics and behavioral patterns associated with one-on-one psychic vampirism. While some of our subjects who scored in the severe range of psychic vampirism were warm and outgoing, others were cold and withdrawn. Several viewed themselves as personally advanced and superior to others. (Such a manifest superiority, of course, could be a reaction to repressed feelings of inadequacy.) In contrast, others viewed themselves as inferior and weak. Many of them tended to be self-absorbed and immature. Other personal traits found among subjects scoring in the severe range were self-doubt, distrust of others, impulsive, low frustration tolerance, and hostility. Jealousy mixed with fear of abandonment often characterized their romantic relationships.

When taken together, our studies identified the following eight categories of one-on-one psychic vampire lifestyles:

1. **The Narcissistic Vampire.** As a group, narcissistic vampires have a grandiose sense of self-importance along with needs for attention and admiration that often reach back to early childhood. They view themselves as superior; however, their self-esteem is usually quite fragile. Their needs for acceptance and recognition drive them to overestimate their accomplishments while either discrediting or taking credit for the work of others. In the work setting, they often seek control of the decision-making process, while exhibiting few of the skills required for responsible decision-making. Lacking empathy, narcissistic vampires tend to disregard the feelings of others while expecting others to be concerned about their welfare. As a group, they tend to be untrustworthy, disdainful, self-absorbed, and self-promoting. Undisciplined and exploitative, they do not hesitate to take advantage of others to achieve their goals. They are often pseudo-intellectuals or con artists with a superficial charm that can be temporarily disarming. They are, as a group, unreliable, critical, and pessimistic. Simplistic and immature in their views of right and wrong, they are quick to judge others. Authoritative and controlling in their social relationships, they have serious difficulty working with people. Their administrative and supervisory skills are extremely limited. They are typically distrustful of colleagues and superiors, as reflected in their excessive demands for documentation ("in writing") of even minor issues. Frequently found in the academic setting, they are often aggressive publicity seekers who embellish and exaggerate their credentials as "scholars." Their claims of

being "skeptical thinkers" are almost always a bid for attention or a reaction to their felt insecurities and shallow intellect. They characteristically react to their own lack of integrity by calling into question the integrity of others. The prognosis for the narcissistic vampire is extremely poor.

2. **The Schizoid Vampire.** In contrast to the narcissistic vampire, schizoid vampires are typically withdrawn and apathetic. They tend to be emotionally detached and uncomfortable in their social interactions except during their isolated vampire episodes. They are usually loners who have few if any close friends. Their romantic relationships are turbulent, fragile, and transient. They typically appear emotionally cold, but underneath their veneer of social indifference are painful feelings of insecurity and isolation.

3. **The Paranoid Vampire.** A major characteristic of this vampire style is suspicion and distrust. Paranoid vampires usually expect the worst from people. They often believe the are being plotted against and exploited. Excessively suspicious and hostile, paranoid vampires scrutinize others in search for hidden meanings behind their remarks and actions. They bear grudges and are slow to forgive even minor slights or criticisms. Because their paranoia consumes enormous amounts of energy, they are among the most active psychic vampires. Often underlying their vampire attacks against others are efforts to either control or punish. They are quick to use vampire assaults for revenge or as counterattacks against persons who angered them or in their views mistreated them in some way. While insensitive to the misfortunes of others, paranoid vampires typically exaggerate their own misfortunes—which they often describe as "horrible."

4. **The Antisocial Vampire.** The antisocial vampire shows a long history of either disregarding or violating the rights of others. As a group, they do not hesitate to use deceit and manipulation to achieve their vampire goals. Typically male, they have a history of violating rules, bullying, and lying. Irresponsible and lacking insight, they tend to blame others

for their misfortunes. Brushes with the law are not uncommon among advanced antisocial psychic vampires.

5. **The Addictive Vampire.** Addictive vampires are usually preoccupied with reliving past vampire episodes and planning future conquests. They excessively and indiscriminately select their victims. In addictive vampirism, the vampire compulsion is motivated not only by urgent energy needs but by the challenge and excitement of the conquest. Similar in some ways to pathological gambling, addictive vampirism typically begins early in adulthood or during periods of excessive stress—including the midlife crisis—with the frequency of their vampire episodes progressively increasingly. As in pathological gambling, a sense of power and control often accompanies addictive vampirism. Sexual addiction also frequently accompanies this vampire lifestyle. Because addictive vampires typically center their lives around their vampire conquests, the prognosis for change is extremely poor.

6. **The Socialized Vampire.** The socialized vampire, on the surface at least, is in sharp contrast to most other forms of one-on-one psychic vampirism. Socially skilled, socialized vampires almost always present themselves as trustworthy, friendly, cooperative, and responsible. On the surface, they seem to respect the rights, feelings, and wishes of others, and they are usually seen as understanding and supportive in their relationships. For the most part, they appear emotionally stable, and they tend to conform to prevailing social norms. They are, however, not reluctant to tap the energy system of others and drain energy from them. Like other psychic vampires, they are usually defensive concerning their vampire tendencies. They tend to minimize the seriousness of their vampire conquests by rationalizing them as simply amusing encounters or harmless diversions. As might be expected, socialized vampires are seldom motivated to seek help in changing their vampire lifestyle.

7. **The Cyberspace Vampire.** The Internet can be seen as a pipe that connects people, and in some instances the pipe is used to draw energy. Cyberspace vampires, as they are called, are

usually experienced socialized psychic vampires who seek to expand their vampire conquests through the Internet. The cyberspace chatroom provides a secure sanctuary in which psychic vampires, should they choose to do so, can remain totally anonymous while acting out their vampire impulses with impunity. Incredible as it may seem, however, sophisticated cyberspace vampires often drop clues to their identity and motivation. They have been known, for instance, to use fictitious names that start with the letter *V*, such as Vince, Val, Vanessa, Vonda, and even Vamp. The use of these clues by experienced cyberspace vampires suggests a need to flirt with self-disclosure, perhaps to add excitement to their vampire conquests. Such clues alone, however, do not conclusively indicate psychic vampirism.

8. **The Ambivalent Vampire.** This category consists primarily of inexperienced vampires who are insecure and distressed. Typically lacking self-confidence, ambivalent vampires struggle for liberation from a compulsion that overpowers their drive for independence and self-sufficiency. They are fearful that they are incapable of functioning without the supportive energy of others. Reluctantly and often with remorse, they vampirize their victims because they see no other alternative in meeting their energy needs. The prognosis for this category of vampirism is quite good.

Aside from identifying specific psychic vampire lifestyles, our studies revealed wide-ranging differences in awareness levels among psychic vampires and their victims during the actual vampire attack. Although the psychic vampire episode can occur subconsciously for both the vampire and victim, the more experienced psychic vampires in our studies were usually aware of the energy infusion process that, typically, they deliberately initiated. Even when the vampire attack seemed to occur effortlessly, the experienced psychic vampire was usually aware of the process. The vampirized victim, on the other hand, was typically unaware of the vampire attack until considerable loss of energy had occurred. Even then, many victims attributed the resultant weakness and fatigue to other factors, such as stress, health issues, and not enough rest or sleep.

As a group, the psychic vampires in our studies were found to be quite resourceful in using all their available options to initiate and maintain their one-on-one vampire interactions. Ironically, the energies many of them expend to meet their vampire needs could be easily redirected to empower their internal energy system and restore its energizing functions. Unfortunately, psychic vampires are almost always motivated by more than the need for energy. It seems that for many experienced psychic vampires, the challenge and excitement of the conquest are equally as important as the energy rewards. Also, many vampire strategies seem to focus more on social needs than energy. The experienced vampire, in particular, is often skilled at manipulating the social situation to establish a trusting relationship that increases their targeted prey's vulnerability and sets the stage for a subtle invasion of the victim's energy system. Incredible as it may seem, several psychic vampires in our studies believed they increased their social status by vampirizing a higher status victim.

But while many psychic vampires seem to need the social interaction as much as the energy infusion, other vampires demonstrate little interest in the social situation. They admit using social interactions simply as means to an end—their primarily objective is not to socialize, but rather to vampirize. They may, in fact, decide to sidestep the social interaction altogether by tapping directly into their unsuspecting victim's energy system. Once connected to their victims, they subtly draw energy from them at a barely noticeable rate until their vampire needs are satisfied. They sometimes select total strangers as their prey.

Often underlying advanced one-on-one vampirism is a blatant disregard for the rights of other, along with a willingness to violate those rights. Many unscrupulous psychic vampires possess a superficial charm, but underneath they tend to be callous and arrogant. They can be at once engaging, perplexing, and disconcerting. Exploitation and deception are common strategies. They ask, "What can I get out of this interaction?" or, "How can I use this interaction to my advantage?" When they help others, it is usually with the expectation that they will receive something in return. They often flatter and charm others to promote themselves. They can stoop to flagrant ingratiation in their relationships with persons who can do something for them. On the surface, they can appear trustworthy and sincere, but underneath they are self-centered and unreliable. When to their advantage, they are not reluctant to betray others, an attribute found among almost all highly advanced psychic vampires.

Because their primary focus is on themselves and their interests, it is extremely difficult for psychic vampires to establish and maintain long-term relationships. Like their folklore counterpart, their vampire needs are a driving force over which they often have little or no control. When frustrated, or in highly threatening situations, they can be intrusive, inconsiderate, and, at times, dangerously aggressive.

Highly advanced psychic vampires of the one-on-one kind, while preoccupied with their own needs, are typically insensitive to the needs of others. Usually lacking integrity, they are almost always devoid of spiritual values, which as seen by them are either irrational or a sign of weakness. They are typically unstable, self-centered, and ready to lie to protect themselves, obtain favors, or advance occupationally. They are characteristically unprincipled and unpredictable in their efforts to satisfy their energy needs.

A history of sexual exploitation is common among highly experienced psychic vampires. Their relationships often include a succession of sexual partners who are seen by them as "objects to be used." A college professor admitted that he derived a surge of rejuvenating energy through his recurrent sexual relationships with much younger partners who were often his students.

The temporary increase in energy experienced by the psychic vampire during a very severe attack can result in a critical loss of energy for the vampirized victim, thus dangerously depleting the normal energy reserve. Even more serious, the victim's self-energizing functions can be so severely interrupted that spontaneous recovery is difficult, thus increasing vulnerability to additional attacks. In cases of repeated attacks, the victim's internal energy system can undergo structural damage sufficient to impair its capacity to replenish the lost energy.

Among host victims, the first signs of a psychic vampire attack are almost always weakness and fatigue, both of which can be either instant or gradual in onset, depending on the nature of the attack. Not surprisingly, victims of a severe attack often report feelings of being "totally drained," both mentally and physically. Among other common physical reactions are dizziness, irregular heartbeat, light-headedness, and sometimes nausea. Victims often describe their reactions as similar to those associated with the loss of blood, sea-sickness, vertigo, or jet lag.

Although the symptoms associated with a single vampire attack are often short-lived, they tend to persist in situations involving regular interactions with an active psychic vampire. The wear-and-tear effects of repeated attacks can include severe anxiety and depression. Common symptoms include sleep disturbances, difficulty concentrating, forgetfulness, irritability, feeling on edge, and loss of interest in daily activities.

Depending on the severity of the attack, victims of a psychic vampire attack often experience a sense of violation during and immediately following the episode. Interestingly, female victims of male vampires frequently report a mild aroma similar to Clorox or onions immediately before and during the attack—a phenomenon which could be related in some way to the folklore notion of garlic as a vampire repellent. In contrast, male victims of a male vampire attack often experience an aroma which they describe as "musty" or "stale." Both male and female victims of the female vampire, on the other hand, often report a mild aroma of mint. In our studies, both male and female victims of a very severe psychic vampire attack commonly reported dryness of mouth along with a taste they described as "bitter." Among other physical reactions associated with a very severe attack are tingling sensations, brief ringing in the ears, and flushed face and neck, to list but a few. While these symptoms are strong signals of a psychic vampire episode, none of them alone conclusively indicates a psychic vampire attack as either impending or underway.

Our studies found that most experienced psychic vampires prefer a close, frontal position for their attacks which often target the victim's solar plexus region. It would follow that, once aware of a possible attack, the potential victim can take the "bite" out of a vampire assault by simply turning and walking away. While spatial distance alone does not provide complete protection, it can limit the severity of the attack. We will later discuss certain fail-safe strategies that, with practice, offer full protection, even when flight is not an option.

Unfortunately, psychic vampire episodes often occur spontaneously with neither the vampire nor victim consciously aware of the attack, particularly when it is mild and the amount of energy transferred is minimal. Even when the energy loss is substantial, the concept of psychic vampirism is often unknown to the victim as well as the vampire. Lacking awareness of the phenomenon, they may seek other plausible explanations for the effects of the attack. The psychic vampire, in such spontaneous situations, may even assume that the interaction is mutually rewarding. The nondiscerning vampire may attribute the new surge of energy following an attack to a satisfying social exchange; whereas the unsuspecting victim may attribute the loss of energy to a flat, boring, or dull interaction. Even when the concept of psychic vampirism is known to both vampire and victim, the vampire may deny any personal vampire tendency; and the victim may deny any sense of personal vulnerability. Whether spontaneous or deliberate, conscious or unconscious, the psychic vampire episode is always one-sided, with the vampire benefiting from the experience at the expense of the vampirized victim.

In studying one-on-one vampirism, I was particularly interested in isolating some of the strategies used by experienced psychic vampires to deliberately initiate and maintain their vampire episodes. Apparently motivated by low energy and a deficient energy system, the psychic vampires in our studies had often but unsuccessfully sought workable ways of meeting their energy needs. Whether male or female, they eventually acquired, often through trial and error, vampire strategies that seemed to work for them personally.

While unknown to them, many of the strategies acquired by highly experienced psychic vampires in our studies were also being used by other experienced vampires. Their strategies were particularly similar in initiating first-time attacks. Subsequent attacks with the same victim apparently required less effort. We found that the experienced vampire usually orchestrates the attack through mental intent to extract energy from a selected victim followed by efforts to control spatial distance. While physical contact is not required, a small spatial distance between vampire and victim seems to facilitate the attack. In social gatherings, the experienced vampire usually targets a victim, moves in slowly, and then briefly turns aside before moving in even more closely for the actual vampire attack, a process so common that we labeled it the preliminary vampire maneuver.

To our surprise, experienced psychic vampires in our studies often showered their target victims with energy just before the actual attack. This may help to explain the resurgence of energy which is commonly experienced among target vampire victims just prior to the onset of fatigue and other symptoms. Feeling refreshed and at ease, the victim is placed off guard and thus made more vulnerable to the impending attack. Although the energizing techniques used by vampires before an attack are somewhat unclear, they usually involve efforts to connect mentally with the potential victim. Common strategies include a disarming smile, positive verbal interaction, fleeting eye contact, and, if convenient, limited physical touch, particularly when the designated target is the other sex. In group discussions, the experienced psychic vampires in our study came up with the term, *vampire foreplay,* to describe the preliminary process that reduced resistance and finally activated the vampire event.

Many of the experienced vampires in our studies saw the vampire attack as an energizing process that could be initiated by simply permitting or "giving in" to it. To facilitate the energy transfer process, they often envisioned a channel connecting them to their victim. They usually sustained the energy infusion until it reached its peak or else the victim's energy reached a critically low level. They were careful not to deplete the energy supply of the host victim to a dangerously low level, which could hinder future interactions. Once initiated, the vampire episode ranged from a few seconds to several minutes. Typically, the attack was terminated through the same strategy that initiated it—mental intent.

Taken together, these findings suggest an important survival function of the human energy system. Deprived of essential resources, the self's internal energy system seeks other survival options. Psychic vampires, rather than correcting their flawed internal energy system, turn to external energy sources—the energy systems of their host victims. This Band-Aid solution is temporary, of course. It not only fails to fix the vampire's flawed energy system, it thwarts the growth process while, at the same time, seriously interfering in the well-being of the host victim.

General versus Couples Vampirism

As indicated by Interactive Questionnaires I and II as previously presented, one-on-one psychic vampirism occurs in two major forms, depending on the designated victim. The first form, which we call *general,* targets victims from the general population; whereas the second form, which we call *couples,* targets victims who are partners in an on-going relationship.

In its general form, psychic vampirism can involve considerable complexity. Except after an extended period of energy deprivation, both men and women psychic vampires tend to be somewhat selective in targeting their victims. While experienced male vampires generally target members of the other sex, experienced female vampires tend to equally target males and females, but only if they are perceived as receptive. Inexperienced vampires of both sexes, however, tend to prey on either men or women who are perceived as receptive or vulnerable. Almost never do psychic vampires admit targeting children as victims.

According to our studies, experienced psychic vampires often develop a fixed pattern of preferences in selecting their host victims. Although there are many exceptions, males generally select victims slightly younger than themselves; whereas females tend to select victims of their own age group or slightly older. Among males in particular, the selection process seems to be strongly influenced by the physical attractiveness of the potential victim. Many of them develop a preference for victims of a given physical feature, with color of hair assuming particular importance for males. Where vampirism is involved, gentlemen do indeed prefer blondes. For female vampires, height of the male victim seems to be an important consideration. Compared to men, however, women tend to be more flexible and varied in selecting their victims, with selection based on a combination of features rather than a single characteristic.

Our case studies of active psychic vampires suggested that parental models often influence the victim selection process. One female vampire in our studies, for instance, insisted that her vampire "conquests," as she called them, were limited to males who, like her father, had gray hair. In another case, a male vampire, by his account, selected only women who were both tall and assertive. As it turned out, his mother was considerably taller and more assertive than his father. These observations, while specific to psychic vampirism, reflect the long-term importance of parent-child relationships, along with the possibility of unresolved Oedipal strivings.

In contrast to general vampirism, couples vampirism occurs between persons in a relationship. Couples vampirism can occur early in the relationship as a part of the interaction, or at any point along the way. When it begins later in the relationship, early signs of psychic vampirism were usually evident in the very early stages of the relationship. Here are some examples of partner relationships that are particularly susceptible if not doomed to psychic vampirism.

The Dependent Relationship. In this relationship, one partner is emotionally insecure and overly dependent on the other. In that context, the dependent partner often becomes either overly nurturing or excessively possessive in order to maintain the relationship. The dependent partner who is overly nurturing inadvertently sets the stage for psychic vampirism by becoming a willing victim who actually reinforces the early signs of vampirism in the relationship. On the other hand, the dependent partner who is excessively possessive often becomes the "clinging vine" vampire whose smothering strategies drain energy from the more secure partner and suck vitality from the relationship. Either of these one-sided dependent relationships is predisposed to psychic vampirism from the start.

The Codependent Relationship. This is, unfortunately, a common pattern in couples relationships in which both partners are excessively dependent upon each other. This pathological relationship is maintained as long as the unhealthy dependency needs of both partners are to some extent satisfied. Not infrequently, codependent relationships involve substance abuse in which one partner becomes the enabler who supports the other partner's dependence on alcohol or other drugs. Codependent relationships are especially prone to psychic vampirism because of the similarities in underlying dynamics. In fact, the codependent relationship could be seen as a blueprint for the development of codependent vampirism in which partners drain energy not only from each other but from the relationship as well. In the early stages of codependent vampirism, the victim is usually the enabler who willingly surrenders energy to the dependent partner; but those roles soon shift with both partners drawing energy from each other, possibly because of the relationship's wear-and-tear on the energy system of each partner. In spite of the devastating effects of the codependent vampirism, partners tend to characterize the vampire interaction as a "love relationship," and are thus usually reluctant to change or terminate it.

The Abusive Relationship. Abusive partner relationships provide fertile grounds for the emergence of psychic vampirism. Like many psychic vampires, the abuser, whether male or female, typically disregards the feelings, rights, and wishes of the abused partner. Vampires in abusive relationships are often arrogant and manipulative, with partner domination their primary goal. They show little or no remorse for their abusive behavior—to the contrary, they often blame their victims, seeing them as having gotten what they deserved. They are usually insensitive, aggressive, and extremely irresponsible. Their primary concern is for "number one." Paradoxically, the vampires in abusive relationships often show a history of having been abused; and they may have themselves been victims of psychic vampirism.

The "Perfect" Relationship. Yet another relationship pattern that is particularly vulnerable to psychic vampirism is the so-called "perfect relationship" in which partners are in denial regarding flaws in the relationship. As "perfect partners," they suppress their negative feelings while fabricating a facade of perfection in the relationship. Drained by the demands of being the "perfect" mate and maintaining the thin veneer that holds their "perfect" relationship together, the partners turn curiously to mutual vampirism in which they drain energy from each other. Each partner becomes both vampire and victim. Ironically, the harder they try to sustain the "perfect" relationship, the more the relationship becomes enfeebled. They become more and more irrational in their beliefs about the relationship—*I must have a perfect relationship; I must do whatever it takes to keep this relationship perfect; I totally belong to my partner; I am nothing without my partner; My partner is perfect in every way, therefore I must be perfect; I am nothing without this relationships.* In the long term, their excessive efforts to preserve the relationship exact a severe toll, which can include overwhelming stress and a host of physical complaints. Not surprisingly, most "perfect" relationships eventually self-destruct.

The Competitive Relationship. These relationships are usually built on the ego needs of partners for success, recognition, status, and wealth. The relationship may begin as productively competitive, with each partner independently pursuing important career or personal goals. But the relationship can become unnecessarily stressed when the success gap between the couple widens, particularly among male/female couples when the female forges ahead of the insecure male.

With the relationship deteriorating, both partners may experience conflict, guilt, frustration, insecurity, and vulnerability—all of which are seminal conditions for psychic vampirism. As the relationship weakens, the less successful partner often taps into the energy system of the high achieving partner. Although the results of such a vampire interaction can be temporarily energizing for the insecure partner, it can spell disaster for the relationship. The successful partner, who often senses the vampire nature of the interaction, begins to perceive the relationship as either no longer viable or even worse, obstructive. A pattern of two-way resentment emerges to further advance vampirism in the relationship. In the absence of intervention, the threatened relationship may further weaken and eventually collapse altogether.

The Arranged Relationship. Deliberately arranged relationships are usually based on certain situational factors, which can include convenience and economic considerations. For instance, it may be financial feasible to share an apartment with a roommate or, at another level, to form a partnership in establishing a business. Although the arranged relationship can be productive and rewarding, it can deteriorate, particularly when the expectations of the partners are unfulfilled or their efforts conflict. Once the arranged relationship become strained, a pattern of vampire domination often emerges in which either partner can assume the assertive role of psychic vampire. The more dominant partner may tap the energies of the less dominant partner as a show of power; or on the other hand, the less dominant partner may assume the vampire role as compensation for less control in the relationship. A sense of resentment, entrapment, and fear of personal loss often fuels the vampire interaction. Once psychic vampirism enters the equation, the relationship usually becomes even more strained until if finally fails.

These are only a few of couples situations that are vulnerable to psychic vampirism. It is important, however, to note that productive social relationships, whether between partners or with people in general, are important because they can fulfill a variety of social needs and enrich the quality of our lives. They can strengthen our coping ability, lead to higher self-esteem, and buffer depression and anxiety. They can add meaning to our existence and help us to meet the challenges of everyday life. Psychic vampirism, on the other hand, is harmful and potentially devastating to any relationships. It can weaken the relationship and eventually drain it of vitality and meaning.

Incredible as it may at first seem, psychic vampirism can occur even in soulmate relationships, which are often considered the ultimate form of person-to-person interaction. Sometimes described as destiny, soulmate relationships are often characterized by a sense relational continuity in which highly meaningful past-life relationships continue beyond death and re-emerge in future lives. Ironically, the long-term nature of the soulmate relationship, along with the obligatory close-ness between soulmates (sometimes described a "state of oneness"), can generate unrealistic expectations and vulnerability in the relation-ship. The goal of each lifetime for all of us is growth and change. While the long-term soulmate relationship can promote growth and provide a measure of comfort and stability, it can also foster exploitation and limit the growth options available through other relationships. A sense of constriction, if not bondage, can emerge in which resentment robs vitality from the relationship. Unfortunately, long-term soulmate part-ners usually have little experience in coping with deterioration in their relationships. Once they begin to drift apart, the less secure partner tends to possessively lock into the energy system of the straying part-ner in an effort to re-establish the soulmate interaction. Possessiveness resulting from fear of abandonment in a soulmate relationship is the first symptom of psychic vampirism. Unless restrained, possessiveness can become the death knell to any relationship.

Amazingly, psychic vampirism between partners can involve the mutual consent of both partners, a phenomenon called *consensual vampirism*. This form of interactive vampirism is often found in the fragile romantic relationship that involves a dominant (and sometimes domineering) partner who assumes the role of vampire, and a weaker partner who willingly becomes the victim, often in a bizarre effort to either strengthen or salvage the relationship. The vampire partner, on the other hand, usually rationalizes the interaction as "mutually gratifying."

Among younger consensual vampire couples, including those found in the college student population, the vampire is typically the male partner; whereas among older consensual vampire couples the vampire is typically the female partner. These findings could be explained from at least two perspectives, the one based on age-related tendencies and the other based on role expectations. Supportive of the age-related point of view, our studies found important age differences in vampire tendencies among males and females, with younger males and older females showing a greater inclination toward psychic vampirism than younger females and older males. From the role expectation perspective, we could assume that younger males and older females are expected to be more assertive in expressing their vampire tendencies than older males and younger females. Based on these explanations, romantic vampirism involving an older female and a much younger male partner would probably be highly competitive, because of their mutual assertiveness in expressing their vampire tendencies. As it turns out, however, the older partner, whether male or female, is more likely to assume the assertive role of psychic vampire.

As an interesting aside, our studies of age differences in marriages found that older men and women (age forty and above) with much younger mates often claimed they were rejuvenated by the marital relationship. Supportive of that claim are research findings that older men or women who marry much younger mates do indeed live longer. These findings could suggest that older men and women who seek long-term relationships with much younger partners are motivated by their vampire impulses to tap the youthful energies of their younger mates. Unlike the older vampire partner in these age-different relationships, the younger vampire victim does not live longer. In summary, we could conclude with a degree of caution that long-term vampire interactions between age-different couples are possibly rejuvenating, but only for the older vampire mate. Perhaps not surprisingly, psychic vampire relationships are always fraught with complications. Vampire relationships involving significant age differences are particularly tenuous and seldom long-term.

While one-on-one psychic vampirism is very common, it is often unheard of or, if known, misunderstood by health care professionals. As a result, the symptoms of psychic vampirism, whether those of the vampire or victim, are almost never recognized in the clinical setting as vampire-related. In a recent survey conducted by the author, of eighty-two health care professionals, including clinical psychologists, counselors, social workers, and physicians in the southeastern United States, only eight were familiar with the term, psychic vampire; and only one (a clinical psychologist) reported having treated a victim of psychic vampirism. In that instance, the patient had already diagnosed her condition before seeking therapy; and psychological treatment consisted primarily of palatable therapy designed to help her feel better. None of the health care professionals reported having treated a psychic vampire, and none reported having been trained to either diagnose or treat psychic vampirism. Except for the assessment procedures developed in our laboratories and presented in this book, there appears to exists at present no objective test for measuring psychic vampirism.

Because the tendency toward one-on-one psychic vampirism is so common, almost everyone can benefit from procedures designed to counteract and protect the internal energy system from it. The two procedures that follow are specifically structured to achieve this important goal. The first procedure focuses on the empowering the energy system within the self; whereas the second procedure focuses on empowerment interactions with the outer cosmos. Both procedures are appropriate for psychic vampirism involving either people in general or couples in relationships.

Energy Activation Procedure

The Energy Activation Procedure is designed to promote a fully functional internal energy system that meets our mental, physical, and spiritual energy needs. The internal energy system is seen as dynamic and developmental in nature. The procedure specifies mental and physical techniques that not only enhance the system's existing functions, they also promote continuous development of the system itself. Here's the procedure.

Step 1. The Energy Center Within. Remind yourself that you are a permanent life-force entity with a powerful energy center deep within yourself. With your eyes closed, visualize that center as the vibrant, luminous core of your being with power to generate and distribute mental, physical, and spiritual growth energy. Think of yourself, along with the energy center within, as a cosmic creation that is constantly evolving.

Step 2. The Power of Consciousness. Focus your conscious awareness on the bright energy core situated in your solar plexus. Let the energies of your conscious awareness gently merge with your internal energy core to activate its powers to generate abundant new energy. Sense the vibrant force of energy building within your solar plexus and slowly radiating new energy into every cell and fiber of your body.

Step 3. Energizing Touch. Place the fingertips of both hand over the energy core at your solar plexus region to further stimulate the balanced flow of revitalizing energy throughout your body. As you hold this touch position, note the tingling sensations in your fingertips, a manifestation of the life-force energy flowing from your central energy system to permeate your total being.

Step 4. Empowerment Affirmation. Affirm: *I am now empowered in mind, body, and spirit. I am energized, protected, and secure. I am empowered to repel psychic vampirism or any other threat to my well-being.* You can add in your own words other specific affirmations related to your personal goals or present life situation.

Step 5. Empowerment Cue. Use the energizing touch gesture as presented in Step 3 at any time to instantly activate the full empowering effects of this procedure.

Because of this procedure's energizing effects on the total energy system, it has a near unlimited range of empowering applications. In my practice, I used the procedure with only minor adaptations in treating victims of psychic vampires as well as psychic vampires themselves. By regularly practicing this procedure, victims of psychic vampires discover their power to repel attacks on their energy system; and psychic vampires discover their capacity to generate the energy required to meet their own energy demands, thus making vampirism unnecessary. This procedure is especially effective when applied to partner relationships with a history of psychic vampirism.

Along a totally different line, this procedure has been highly effective in the college setting when used to improve academic performance. Upon revising the procedure to include specific affirmations related to their academic goals, college students who regularly used the procedure dramatically increased their grade-point averages. The procedure has been equally effective in the clinical setting, particular in pain management situations. When practiced regularly, it effectively reduced chronic pain and, in some instances, extinguished it altogether. In whatever the setting it is used, the procedure tends to produce certain general empowering effects, including but not limited to increased self-esteem, a more optimistic outlook, and more productive social interactions. These wide-ranging benefits reflect the critical importance of an empowered, revitalized energy system.

Antennae Activation Strategy

Our hands are critical mechanisms for interacting with our physical environment. Thus it should come as no surprise that some of our most effective self-empowerment procedures utilize the hands as powerful instruments for interacting with other dimensions of reality. The Antennae Activation Strategy uses our hands as the body's antennae with power to link us to the unlimited resources of higher realms of power. Similar in some ways to the Handclasp of Power as discussed earlier in this book, the Antennae Activation Strategy is designed to bring the energy system within each of us into a state of complete congruence with the outer cosmic system of unlimited power. In that state of oneness with the cosmos, we have full access to the boundless resources of that higher dimension which remains the perpetual, energizing force that sustains our existence.

Like the Energy Activation Procedure, this strategy is both versatile and powerful. It is recommended for the host victim (or potential host victim) of psychic vampirism as well as for the psychic vampire in search of self-sufficiency and complete liberation from vampirism. Anyone, in fact, who practices this procedure can be energized and empowered by it. We can all benefit from a closer connection to the higher creative force that underlies the cosmos with its complex matrix of dimensions and planes. By coming into congruence with that force and the cosmos that is energized by it, we can become empowered with unlimited possibilities for growth and greatness. Vampirism has no power over us when we are in that ultimate state of oneness within ourselves and with the higher cosmos. Here is the procedure.

Step 1. Inner Awareness. With your eyes closed, clear your mind of active thought, and then turn your attention inward. Focus on the innermost region of your physical body, and think of that region as the energy core of your being.

Step 2. Oneness Within. Let your thoughts blend with that inner core of bright energy until you experience a sense of oneness with it. With your conscious awareness centered at that quiet core of your being, let the bright energies generated at that region spread gently outward in all directions. Sense the powerful energies as they are absorbed into every fiber of your being. Let them continue to spread outward until you are fully infused and enveloped with powerful, invigorating energy. Note again the wondrous sense of oneness within.

Step 3. Cosmic Sending. As you think of your hands as your body's antennae with powerful sending capacities, turn your palms upward and let the energies of your being go forth into the cosmos. Remind yourself that your internal energy system is made stronger by simply generating and sending energy. As you send energy beyond yourself, sense the clearing of your energy channels. Let all previously blocked, constricted channels become open and fully functional. As your hands remain turned upward, note the warm, tingling sensations in your palms as you send forth powerful energy into the cosmos.

Step 4. Cosmic Contact. You are now in contact with the higher cosmos. Note the wondrous sense of liberation from all your cares. As energy goes forth from you being, all the worries and stresses of life now seem far, far away. You are now empowered with renewed confidence in yourself and your ability to reach beyond to embrace the distant reaches of the cosmos.

Step 5. Cosmic Receiving. As your palms remain turned upward and with your sending mechanisms now fully functional, think of your hands as powerful receiving antennae. Having sent powerful energy into the cosmos, you are now ready to receive. All the abundant resources of the universe are now available to you to enrich and empower your life. Sense powerful, vibrating cosmic energy as it enters your palms and interacts with the central energy system deep within yourself. Note the pulsating infusion of cosmic energy at the very center of your being. As your innermost energy system interacts with the cosmos, you are renewed and empowered with bright, cosmic energy.

Step 6. Cosmic Congruency. Relax your hand and note the profound power within yourself as well as your sense of connection to the higher cosmos. Think of your hands as representing two energy systems—the one within yourself and the other in the higher cosmos. Bring your hands together, palm against palm, as a symbol of congruency and oneness of the two system. As you hold the praying hands position, affirm: *I am now fully attuned and balanced with the cosmos. My total being is energized and empowered. All the resources I need are now at my command.*

Step 7. Antennae Activation Cue. You can access at any time the abundant energy resources, both within yourself and the higher cosmos, by simply bringing your hands together, palm against palm, and affirming: *I am fully energized, attuned, and balanced.* By using this simple cue, you will experience not only the power you need at the moment; but also the sense of personal well-being that consistently accompanies the gesture.

Almost everyone who uses this strategy experiences at once a new burst of energy and power. Following a few practice sessions using the full procedure, you will find that the simple Antennae Activation Cue (Step 7) is sufficient to generate a tranquil state of balance and oneness with the cosmos. This gesture can be used almost anywhere to ward off the threat of psychic vampirism or any other negative force that threatens your well-being.

Even psychic vampires report success in using the Antennae Activation Strategy for overcoming their psychic vampire tendencies and building a strong internal energy system. As we will discover later in this book, many psychic vampires are dissatisfied and guilt-ridden—they desperately seek liberation from vampirism that in some instances has driven them for years to depend on the energy systems of others. For active psychic vampires who are motivated to overcome their vampire compulsions, what better solution than the discovery of unlimited energy resources within not only themselves but also the higher cosmos, just waiting to be used? When we tap into this combination of resources, the possibilities are simply unlimited. Active psychic vampires, like others who practice the procedure, almost always experience a new surge of energy far beyond anything they had imagined. With regular practice of the procedure, they soon become self-empowered, self-energized, and fully liberated.

This strategy, not unlike other procedures presented throughout this book, is applicable to a wide range of personal empowerment goals. It is especially effective as a supportive procedure for breaking unwanted habits, managing stress, overcoming phobias, and coping with anxiety and depression. For these and other applications, the strategy can be easily modified to include powerful goal-related imagery and relevant affirmations.

Summary

One-on-one psychic vampirism is a common but complex phenomenon in which the psychic vampire taps the energy resources of a selected host victim. In survey after survey, a majority of respondents reported past vampire-like social encounters that left them fatigued and low on energy.

In this chapter, we examined the underlying mechanics associated with one-on-one psychic vampirism, and presented tests for measuring psychic vampire tendencies involving people in general as well as couples in relationships. We examined the personal traits associated with one-on-one psychic vampirism and identified a variety of psychic vampire lifestyles. We discussed certain types of partners relationships that seem particularly susceptible if not doomed to psychic vampirism.

Finally, we offered two step-by-step empowerment strategies relevant to one-on-one psychic vampirism. The Energy Activation Procedure is designed to promote a more fully functional internal energy system while promoting continuous development of the system through certain mental and physical techniques. The Antennae Activation Strategy is designed to link us to the cosmic realms of unlimited energy and bring the internal energy system into a state of congruence with the higher cosmos. Both strategies have wide-ranging applications. They are effective empowerment and protection procedures for victims as well as potential victims of psychic vampires; they are also effective for psychic vampires who are motivated to build a strong internal energy system sufficient to liberate them from psychic vampirism.

FOUR

Psychic Vampirism
and the Human Aura

THE HUMAN AURA is a complex component of a larger energy system. As an external energy phenomenon enveloping the physical body, it is a visible manifestation of the energy system's central core situated in the body's solar plexus region. Together, the visible aura and its internal core make up an energy system that is connected to the cosmic life-force sustaining our mental, physical, and spiritual existence.

The human aura is important to our study of psychic vampirism for several reasons. First, the aura is an interactive élan vital that is essential to our personal evolution and well-being. Mentally, physically, and spiritually, we interact with our aura; and the aura, in turn, interacts with other human aura systems. When unprotected, the aura is highly susceptible to psychic vampirism; but when protected and empowered, it is our first line of defense against psychic vampirism. Thanks to years of research, we now know enough about the human aura to maximize its functions and effectively use it, not only as a shield against vampirism, but as an invaluable growth resource as well.

In this chapter, we will first explore the nature of the human aura system and examine its relevance to psychic vampirism. We will then develop ways of viewing and interpreting the aura. Finally, we will present ways of empowering the aura and using it as a resource to promote our personal growth.

The Nature of the Aura System

No two human aura systems are exactly alike. The external aura, along with its energizing core and structural components, is distinctively different for each individual. Even in instances of identical multiple births, each aura systems is unique in cosmic design and function. Among the distinguishing characteristic of the human aura are wide-ranging variations in color, brightness, structural features, frequency levels, and magnitude or expansiveness, each of which provides an index into the aura's developmental level and functions.

Incredible as it may seem, the human aura system provides a cumulative cosmic record of our lives from the very beginning of our existence. Even before our first incarnation, we existed as a unique life-force entity whose destiny was growth and greatness. Our multiple past lifetimes, and the discarnate growth intervals between them, are all recorded in the aura as components of a master cosmic plan. Even the future is reflected in the aura as growth possibilities. As our link to the cosmos, the aura system is the energizing vehicle through which we can access all the unlimited resources of the cosmos and thus achieve our highest potentials.

The human aura, as typically seen, envelops the full body and expands outward from a few inches to several feet. Conceivably, however, the energies of the aura extend far beyond these visible limits, possibly reaching into infinity. If the aura is our contact to the cosmos, it follows that its reaches would indeed be limitless. Unfortunately, we are all too often out of touch with the cosmos and unattuned to its powerful frequencies—conditions that not only impair the aura system's functions; they also increase our vulnerability to psychic vampirism.

The colors found in the human aura can include all the variations of the color spectrum, even those not visible to the human eye. Typically, the aura will consist of a predominant color along with certain other color combinations. The predominant color is usually a brightly energized sphere or rim of color that envelops the full body. It can exist, however, as a somewhat less expansive body of color situated anywhere in the aura, such as in an upper region. Occasionally, the aura will consist of layers of color enveloping the full body, a phenomenon sometimes called the *rainbow aura.* The bright rainbow aura is typically highly developed, attuned, and balanced. It is a characteristic often found in the auras of leaders and humanitarians. Using numerological strategies to determine aura colors of historical figures, our studies found that George Washington and William Shakespeare each had rainbow auras (see my book *Aura Energy for Health, Healing and Balance*). While psychic vampirism can occur in persons with auras of almost any color or color combination, the bright rainbow aura is seldom found among active psychic vampires.

Each color found in the human aura, along with the brightness of the coloration, signals certain personal characteristics. Bright yellow is associated with high intelligence and social skills; whereas dull yellow is associated with obstructions in intellectual and social functioning. Bright green in the aura is associated with healing energies and self-fulfillment; dull green, on the other hand, is associated with illness or frustration. Pink in the aura signals rejuvenation, sensitivity, and altruism; whereas purple suggests abstract and philosophical interests. Orange is often found in the auras of entrepreneurs and high achievers. Brown in the aura is associated with practicality, stability, independence, and outdoor interests. Bright blue is associated with tranquillity and balance; whereas dull blue is associated with anxiety and depression. The common expression, "I feel blue," may reflect an intuitive awareness of dull blue energy in the aura—after all, we visually perceive the world through the lens of the enveloping aura.

Red in the aura, a relatively rare color usually signifying an intense emotional state, is particularly relevant to our study of psychic vampirism. Flashes of red are common in the auras of highly aggressive psychic vampires, particularly just before or during an attack. As a general rule, the auras of active psychic vampires are dull or dingy in color. Blotches of dull greenish gray, typically considered a foreboding color when found anywhere in the aura, are typical in the auras of full-blown psychic vampires. They are especially common in the abdominal or chest regions of advanced psychic vampires.

Like coloration, the structural makeup of the aura varies widely from person to person. As in color, the aura's specific structural patterns signify certain related personal traits. Here are some examples of structural characteristics and their relevance to psychic vampirism.

Streams of energy, sometimes called *streamers*, are veins of energy that usually radiate outward but can meander throughout the aura. Like the physical body's circulatory system, they are essential to the healthy aura in distributing energy throughout the aura system. Almost invariably, very few active streams of energy are found in the auras of psychic vampires. Aura empowerment procedures, as we will later see, can be structured to open blocked energy pathways and promote the free flow of life-force energy.

Clusters of energy are intermeshing networks of energy typically found in the aura's outer regions. Clusters are concentrations of energy that meet specific energy needs, such as protecting or energizing a particular region in the aura system. The color of the cluster can provide a key to its empowerment role. For instance, bright green clusters are distributors of healing energy whereas pink clusters are associated with rejuvenation. Although bright clusters of energy are common in the typical aura, they are seldom seen in the auras of psychic vampires. When discolored or dark clusters appear, particularly within the constricted aura, they almost always signal psychic vampirism. We will later explore ways of adding bright clusters of color to the aura.

Points of bright energy in the aura suggest highly specialized empowerment functions, including the presence of a spiritual entity or guide, particularly when an unusually bright point occurs somewhere beyond the area of normal aura activity. Typically, the brighter and larger the point, the greater its empowering potential. I have never seen points of energy in the auras of active psychic vampires. Effective strategies for introducing points of bright energy into the aura have not yet been developed.

Points of darkness are associated with either a weakness in the aura or a puncture wound resulting from a psychic vampire attack. When associated with a vampire attack, points of darkness are usually surrounded by grayish discoloration suggesting a localized deficiency of energy. Points of darkness are sometimes surrounded by dark strands, which are conceivably vampire filament left over from a recent attack. As vampire residue, these dark strands can function temporarily as a vampire virus that may infiltrate the full aura and further drain it of energy. We will later discuss in greater detail the vampire virus and ways of counteracting it.

Voids are inactive, nonfunctional regions in the aura. As wasted space, they signal a sluggish aura along with vulnerability to external threats, including psychic vampirism. Psychic vampires, along with their victims, often show serious voids in their auras. Later in this chapter, we will discuss ways of filling voids in the aura.

Agitation is a churning turbulence in the aura. When accompanied by discoloration, agitation in the aura suggests anxiety, depression, or fear; but when accompanied by brightness, it signals an urgent mobilization of the aura's energy resources in meeting a particularly demanding situation. The psychic vampire, when poised for an attack, invariably shows discolored agitation in the aura. Effective strategies, including the aura massage, have been developed to alleviate aura agitation and replace it with balance.

Symmetry is characterized by a balanced distribution of energy throughout the aura. The symmetrical aura suggests attunement to the higher cosmos. Strategies that generate symmetry and attunement in the aura provide an excellent defense against psychic vampirism.

Fissures are irregular, jagged breaks or tears in the aura. When surrounded by dull discoloration, they are thought to be the result of abuse or psychic trauma. Fissures are common in the auras of psychic vampires. They are sometimes seen in the auras of victims of a recent psychic vampire attack.

Tentacles are dark, sharp-pointed elongations that reach beyond the aura's normal external boundaries. This pattern is almost always found in the auras of active psychic vampires. Vampire tentacles are elastic and can be extended to considerable distances to puncture the aura of a host victim and suck energy from it. Vampire tentacle attacks can inflict serious damage to the victim's aura, including puncture wounds and deep lacerations. Vampire tentacles are visible through certain aura viewing strategies as well as electrophotographic procedures, as we will later discover.

Arcs are bright rays of energy that connect two aura systems. Unlike tentacles that invade another aura, arcs indicate positive energy interactions. They are often found in the auras of couples whose relationship is fulfilling. Arcs are also observed during psychic healing as vehicles for the transfer of healing energy from one aura to another.

Halos are glowing perimeters of energy enveloping the total aura. As a bright enveloping sphere of intense energy, the halo is one of our best protections against psychic vampire invasions. The Finger Interlock Procedure, which we will later discuss, is one of the best procedures known for instantly erecting a protective halo of energy around the full aura. Once the full procedure is mastered, the simple finger interlock cue can be used almost anywhere to prevent a vampire attack, or once an attack is in progress, to promptly end it.

Symmetrical energy forms are bright concentrations of energy in a variety of symmetrical shapes found typically in the upper regions the aura. Symmetrical forms in the aura generate powerful energies that promote healthy mental and spiritual growth. Among the most common forms are bright orbs and pyramids. Bright green orbs, which are believed to generate healing energy, are often found in the auras of health care professionals and gifted psychic healers alike. The pyramid is associated with psychic insight and cosmic attunement. Highly symmetrical energy forms are seldom found in the auras of active psychic vampires.

Aura Photography

Among the important benchmarks in the study of the human aura are the early contributions of Russian scientists, Semyon and Valentina Kirlian. Their electrophotographic process known as *Kirlian* or *corona-discharge photography* was hailed by many scientists as a way to see the invisible, and a window to the unknown. Several American scientists concluded that the Kirlians had photographed life-force energy, thereby providing a totally new approach for exploring the human energy system.

Inspired by the Kirlian studies, my research efforts using electrophotography included controlled laboratory studies funded by the U.S. Army, the Parapsychology Foundation of New York, and several private sources. Initiated in 1976 at Athens State University, my early studies of the aura focused primarily on the corona-discharge patterns surrounding the right index fingertip. Although other highly useful aura photographic procedures are now available, limiting my early research efforts to photographic recordings of the right index fingertip provided an experimental condition in which appropriate controls could be introduced. The experimental set-up included a pressure control and finger orientation device we designed specifically for our studies (see Figure 1, below). The device was important to our research because it provided constant control of finger orientation as well as pressure applied to the fingertip as it rested upon the film during the photo shoot.

With these controls in place, the photographs provided a cross-section of the aura enveloping the fingertip. Repeated fingertip photographs of the same individual over an extended period of time showed a high consistency of aura patterns, including but not limited to such features as voids, streamers, fissures, and clusters. Because the aura pattern around the fingertip is a relatively stable phenomenon, we call it the person's *aura signature.*

Equally as profound as the stable aura pattern found in the repeated fingertip photographs for a given individual was the discovery that the aura signature found in the photographs of the right index fingertip is fairly representative of the individual's full aura, a

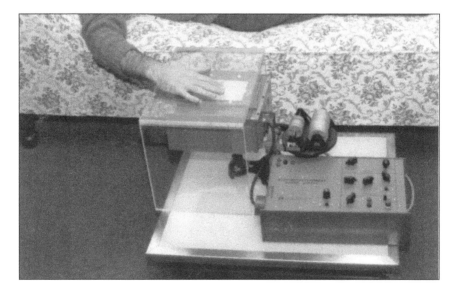

FIGURE 1. EXPERIMENTAL SET-UP FOR AURA PHOTOGRAPHY.

conclusion based on comparisons of the individual's fingertip photographs and the results of full aura viewings by trained specialists. For instance, when such features as clusters and voids when found in the fingertip photographs, they were likewise present in the full aura. When we stop to consider that the fingers are antennae for the body, the strong similarity found in the aura patterns around the fingertip and the full aura becomes quite plausible.

Psychic Vampirism and the Aura

The photographic results of these early research efforts included several important finding related to psychic vampirism. As a research strategy, aura photography offers a convenient, objective procedure for identifying psychic vampirism and evaluating the effects of procedures designed to protect and empower the aura, as we will later discover in this chapter.

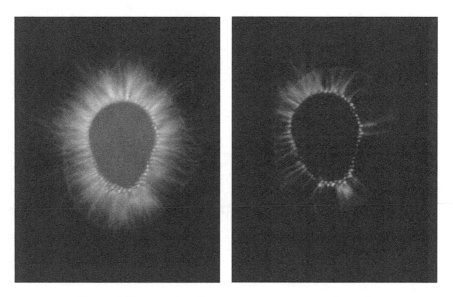

FIGURE 2. EXPANSIVE (LEFT) VERSUS CONSTRICTIVE AURA (RIGHT).

One of the most common features associated with psychic vampirism is the severely constricted aura (see Figure 2, previous page). Among subjects who showed severe tendencies toward vampirism on the interactive questionnaires as discussed in the previous chapter, the photographic pattern around the fingertip almost invariably showed a severely constricted aura. The constricted aura suggests a deficiency in available energy resources as well as an underdeveloped internal energy system, both of which are predisposing factors related to psychic vampirism.

Another feature commonly associated with psychic vampirism is the *vampire shadow phenomenon* (see Figure 3, inset below). This pattern is characterized by a shadowy outer region enveloping the aura accompanied by unusually long tentacles that reach beyond the normal aura boundary. As already noted, the aura around the fingertip provides a highly reliable index into the full aura. It is thus not surprising to find that when either a constricted pattern or the vampire shadow phenomenon appears in fingertip photographs, it is almost always present in the full aura.

While vampire tentacles function primarily to suck energy from the host victim, they can inflict serious damage to the aura. During the psychic vampire attack, tentacles can often be observed either interfacing the host victim's aura or actually puncturing or hooking into it, sometimes from considerable distances. When tentacles interface the victim's aura, they seem to slowly absorb energy from it; but when they penetrate the aura, they can rapidly exhaust the aura's energies. A sharp tentacle penetration typically results in a dark puncture wound to the

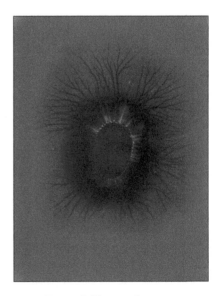

FIGURE 3. VAMPIRE SHADOW PHENOMENON.

aura; whereas a tentacle snag causes serious, uneven tears or fissure wounds that spill energy from the aura. A jagged tear to the aura is associated with an intensely aggressive vampire attack deliberately designed to inflict damage.

Many victims of vampire puncture assaults on the aura report momentarily piercing pain at the area of damage to the aura; whereas a sharp stinging sensation often accompanies vampire attacks that inflict tears to the aura. These immediate, localized sensations are typically followed by residual discomfort that can continue for several days.

Incredible as it may at first seem, vampire attacks not only inflict puncture wounds and lacerations to the aura, they can also result in small, dark strands similar to isolated streamers at the site of the attack as well. Believed to be fragments of the vampire's aura, the dark strands are at first observed around open aura wounds that were inflicted by vampire tentacles. But once implanted at the site of injury, they can spread rapidly throughout the victim's aura to result in the so-called *vampire virus*. When they occur in fingertip photographs, the virus fragments are usually visible in dark relief throughout the aura. Always incompatible with the victim's aura, the vampire fragments feed like a parasite on the victim's aura to further consume its energies.

Among the common effects of the vampire virus are, as might be expected, low energy and fatigue, but beyond that an ominous awareness that something is awry. Anxiety and a menacing sense of helplessness soon emerge as the aura takes on an ominous greenish-gray overlay. Fortunately, the virus is not contagious, and its effects are usually short-lived. Even in the absence of intervention, the vampire fragments usually dissolve and the related symptoms disappear within a few days—that is, unless another vampire attack occurs. Should the virus and its accompanying symptoms persist, they can be promptly extinguished through intervention procedures that energize and illumine the aura.

Unfortunately, in certain couples' relationships, vampirism is an ongoing phenomenon in which one partner habitually drains energy from the other. In the more serious cases, the vampire attack can inflict serious structural damage to the aura that may require a very long recovery period. Victims of an abusive relationship, in particular, often show serious tears in the aura. Aside from damage to their aura, victims coming out of the relationship are almost always burdened by painful emotional residue, which typically includes anxiety, distrust, and reluctance to enter another relationship. The vampire partner, on the other hand, is usually preoccupied with finding another vulnerable victim.

Highly effective strategies, which we will later discuss, are now available for viewing the aura and observing the effects of vampire onslaughts. Increasingly, enlightened counselors and therapist everywhere are using aura-related skills for both diagnosis and therapy (though not necessarily for conditions related to psychic vampirism). As a practicing psychologist, I have often observed damage to the aura, especially among persons in severely distressful relationships. Severe puncture wounds and deep, uneven tears inflicted to punish or control are particularly common.

Since psychic vampirism is so rampant in troubled relationships, and because main-line therapy approaches are often insufficient in resolving vampire-related issues in couples therapy, I have incorporated into my clinical practice a program called Aura Orientation and Training. Included in the program are techniques that guide couples, not only in solving problems, but also in mastering appropriate aura intervention and protection strategies. Equipped with new insight and workable self-empowerment options, they emerge from therapy with a sense of accomplishment and personal power, changes which are readily evident as renewed brightness and expansiveness throughout their auras.

Occasionally appearing in electrophotographs of the aura is a pattern known as the *remote-image phenomenon* (Figure 4, following page). Consisting of a small point of glowing energy outside the normal range of aura activity, the remote-image phenomenon suggests the presence of a higher plane guide or guardian angel. A cluster of very bright energy within the area of normal aura activity, a phenomenon known as the *luminous cluster phenomenon,* also suggests the presence of higher plane influences. Figure 5, shown below, shows a very rare combination of the luminous cluster as seen at the top of the photograph and the halo effect, which consists of an outer ring of energy enveloping the aura pattern, a phenomenon we will later discuss. When either the remote image or cluster of bright energy appears in photographs of the fingertip, other manifestations of a guiding presence typically occur in other regions of the person's full aura. Examples are a glowing orb of bright energy, which usually appears externally to the aura, typically around the head or shoulder region.

The remote-image phenomenon occurred recently in the aura of an undergraduate student who was a volunteer participant in a privately funded study designed to investigate the stability of the aura's color patterns. The study required daily aura photographs of the right index fingertip of each research subject over a six-week period. Upon reporting late for a scheduled photograph during the fourth week of the study, he explained the delay as the result of a

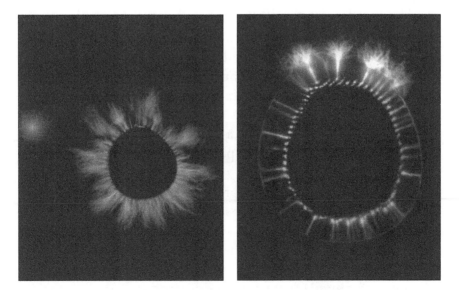

FIGURE 4 (LEFT). THE REMOTE-IMAGE PHENOMENON.
FIGURE 5 (RIGHT). THE LUMINOUS CLUSTER PHENOMENON AND HALO EFFECT.

near accident on a winding road just outside the city. By his account, as he approached a sharp curve, he became suddenly aware of a spiritual presence accompanied by a hand resting on his shoulder and a clear message to drive slowly. He instantly applied his breaks and barely avoided crashing into a stalled vehicle on the narrow bridge just around the sharp curve. Upon obtaining his aura photograph, I immediately noted a bright point of light clearly visible for the first time in the external region of his corona-discharge pattern. Elated at the sight of the bright image, he explained it as an unmistakable manifestation of his ministering guide who had been his protector since childhood. The remote image appeared in his aura photographs over the next several days.

Bright points or clusters of energy can appear in the aura not only at times of potential danger, but also during particularly difficult periods or complex transition, such as the loss of a job or break-up of a relationship. Points of light as well as luminous clusters, rather than ominous warnings, are bright manifestations of affection and protection. They reveal the presence and support of caring cosmic helpers, while reminding us of the limitless possibilities around us. Through simply becoming aware of these cosmic influences, we can become energized and more fully empowered. A military photographer who assisted in my early research noted the appearance of a bright cluster of energy in his aura following the unexpected death of his father in an accident. Aware of the significance of the phenomenon that remained in his aura for several weeks, he valued the cluster as a clear indication of a comforting spiritual presence at his time of personal loss.

There is strong evidence to suggest that the color of remote images and clusters in the aura provide a reliable index to their purposes or empowerment functions. Iridescent green points and clusters, for instance, almost always signal healing energy. When found in the auras of the seriously ill, they usually remain present throughout the recovery period and sometimes well beyond. When found in the auras of mentally distressed or grieving persons, they suggest the nurturing support of higher plane entities. As noted earlier, bright green as a dominant color in the full aura typically suggests an abundance of healing energy. It is the color found most frequently in the auras of health care professionals as well as gifted psychic healers.

Higher plane resources, as we will later discover, are among our best defenses against psychic vampirism. But more than providing protection, they enable us to stretch our limits and reach totally new levels of growth and enlightenment. Given access to the rich resources of higher cosmic planes, we can reach beyond our current limits and discover totally new meaning to our lives.

Viewing the Aura

The ability to see the aura is critically important to our study of psychic vampirism. Like aura photography, viewing the aura directly can help to identify active psychic vampirism or the potential for it, while suggesting appropriate intervention strategies. For instance, viewing the aura can detect specific areas of vulnerability or weakness—such as breaks and voids—while prescribing ways of correcting them. Aura viewing can also detect the highly constricted aura, a very common condition that, as already noted, suggests a distinct inclination toward psychic vampirism. Typically energy deficient, the constricted aura indicates a weak, stressed system with very few vampire defense properties.

Aside from its diagnostic and treatment applications, aura viewing is a critical component of strategies designed to access higher cosmic energy sources, the ultimate in aura empowerment. By interacting with the cosmic dimension of life-force energy, we can access a bountiful supply of energy in its purest, most powerful form. Once connected, attuned, and balanced to that dimension, we become fully empowered and totally protected from the onslaught of psychic vampirism or any other negative force. Through aura viewing, we can actually see the effects of these strategies on the aura as they occur.

In our laboratory, we used aura viewing regularly in developing the intervention and protection procedures that follow in this chapter. By viewing the aura before, after, and sometimes during the implementation of a given procedure, we were able to revise and fine-tune the procedure to increase its effectiveness. Our studies consistently showed that seeing the effects of a procedure for oneself actually increased the procedure's effectiveness. Perhaps not surprisingly then, aura viewing is often included as an integral component of aura empowerment procedures.

A wide range of aura-viewing strategies is available for viewing one's own aura as well as the auras of others. Among the most effective viewing strategies are the Peripheral Gaze Procedure for viewing the aura of others and the Aura Hand-viewing Procedure for viewing one's own aura. For both procedures, natural daylight or soft, indirect lighting and a neutral background are recommended for practice purpose. A single practice session using either of these procedures is usually sufficient to bring the aura, with its colors and other distinguishing features, into full focus. Each procedure requires only seconds to implement. Once mastered, these viewing strategies can be used under almost any condition.

The Peripheral Gaze Procedure

Developed in our laboratories, this procedures generates a phenomenon known as the *white-out effect* to bring the aura enveloping the full body of another person into view. The white-out effect is an optical illusion consisting of a milky-white glow produced around an object by first gazing directly at the object and then slowly expanding peripheral vision to its limit. The Peripheral Gaze Procedure uses the subject's forehead as the point of focus for producing the white-out effect, which is then replaced by the colorful glow of the aura, typically within seconds. Attention can then be shifted directly to the aura and its various features, including color and structural features.

For this procedure, the person to be viewed is situated at a distance of about ten feet from the viewer and approximately two feet away from an off-white, nonglossy background wall or screen. Here is the procedure.

Step 1. Relaxation. Before viewing the aura, take a few moments to let yourself become progressively relaxed by mentally scanning your body, beginning at your forehead and slowly progressing downward. Visualize a soft glow accompanying your scan and infusing your body with relaxation. Pause briefly at areas of tightness or tension, and let them absorb the soft glow of relaxation. Continue the scan until the glow of relaxation envelops your total body, then silently affirm: *I am now fully relaxed.*

Step 2. Peripheral Gaze. Gaze for a few moments at your subject's forehead, and then slowly expand your peripheral vision to take in your subject's full surroundings. Once your peripheral vision reaches its limits, let your eyes fall slightly out of focus. You will then experience the white-out effect in which your subject is surrounded by a milky-white glow.

Step 3. Aura Focusing. Bring your eyes back into focus and again gaze at your subject's forehead. Almost immediately, the aura will become visible.

Step 4. Aura Viewing. You are now ready to focus your attention on your subject's aura and its myriad of characteristics, including coloration, expansiveness, and structural features. Should your eyes tire during viewing, either close them for a moment or look briefly into the distance away from your subject. If the aura begins to fade during the viewing, close your eyes briefly and repeat the full procedure.

The Peripheral Gaze Procedure is highly effective for people who have never seen the human aura, or else have difficulty perceiving color in the aura. In their efforts to view the aura using other strategies, those who report seeing only a colorless glow around the subject are probably experiencing the white-out effect. Through the Peripheral Gaze Procedure, they are usually successful in progressing to the next level where they perceive the full aura with its colors and other distinguishing characteristics for the first time.

The Peripheral Gaze Procedure is an invaluable aid in identifying damage to the aura resulting from a psychic vampire attack. A

localized dark spot anywhere in the aura is almost always an indication of a "vampire hit" in which the aura was punctured and
energy drawn from it. Also, dark fissures and open incisions in the
aura can signal a seriously damaging attack. Jagged fissures are
often the result of an invading vampire's hook-like tentacle snag-
ging the aura and literally tearing it. Smooth incision wounds, on
the other hand, can signify an attack in which a sharp, blade-like
vampire tentacle deliberately cuts into the aura to spill energy from
it. Both fissures and cuts to the aura are often the results of violent
attacks that seem primarily designed to harm the aura rather than
simply extract energy from it. These serious damages to the aura
are usually inflicted by vindictive psychic vampires who are driven
by jealousy or revenge. In the absence of appropriate intervention,
fissures and cuts to the aura can become long-term wounds that
drain essential energies from the aura system, even in the absence
of additional vampire assaults.

The Aura Hand-viewing Procedure

Viewing one's own aura is relevant to psychic vampirism because it
can identify deficiencies in the aura and suggest appropriate intervention procedures. But viewing one's own aura, and equally as
important, interpreting its characteristics, require a structured procedure that is both objective and reliable. The Aura Hand-viewing
Procedure meets that demand. Developed in our laboratories, this
procedure is based on studies that included comparisons of self-
viewing results with aura photographic recordings as well as the
aura viewings of trained specialists. As a result, the Aura Hand-viewing Procedure is one of the most highly researched and reliable
strategies available today for viewing one's personal aura as it
appears around the hand and lower arm.

If, as already noted, patterns observed in aura photographs of the
right index fingertip are generally representative of the full aura, it
would follow that the aura enveloping the full hand and lower arm
would provide an even stronger index into the nature of the full aura. A
constricted aura around the hand and arm would thus signal a con-

stricted aura around the total body. Similarly, a turbulent aura around the hand and arm would be a strong indication of turbulence throughout the total aura system. Such specific features as voids, streamers, and clusters, when found in the aura around the hand and arm, would suggest similar features in other regions of the aura as well.

The Aura Hand-viewing Procedure requires only a few seconds to bring the aura into view. Here is the procedure.

Step 1. Relaxation. Take in a few deep breaths and exhale slowly as you clear your mind of all active thought. Give yourself permission to become increasingly relaxed, beginning with the muscles in the forehead and then flowing gently downward to infuse your total body with relaxation.

Step 2. Finger Spread. Extend either hand and hold it, palm side outward, at arm's length with your fingers spread slightly against a nonglaring, off-white background.

Step 3. Visualization. Visualize a small dot floating in the space between your thumb and index finger.

Step 4. Gazing. Gaze at the imaginary dot until the aura appears, first as a whitish glow around your thumb and index finger, and then in color around your hand and lower arm. Should you tire during this step, take a few moments to relax and then resume gazing.

Step 5. Aura Viewing. Shift your gaze from the imaginary dot directly to the aura and note its unique characteristics. Pay particular attention to the aura's coloration, structural features, and expansiveness.

Our studies found that simply viewing the aura, whether one's own or that of another person, tends to stimulate our inner resources, including our psychic faculties. Gifted psychics often gaze at their subject's aura before a reading as a means of activating their extrasensory powers, including clairvoyance, precognition, and telepathy. Many psychic healers routinely use aura viewing as a component of the healing process, particularly when it includes efforts to infuse the subject's aura with new healing energies.

Once the aura is visible, a variety of intervention procedures can be readily implemented.

Aura Intervention

As already noted, a constricted aura is among the major characteristics associated with psychic vampirism. Unfortunately, the constricted aura suggests a two-edged vulnerability: (1) It is an easy target for a psychic vampire assault because it possesses few if any vampire resistance or defense properties; and (2) people with this aura characteristic have little energy to spare, and are thus unfortunately prone to becoming psychic vampires themselves. Any condition that further weakens the aura—financial reversal, physical illness, mental distress, painful transitions, and so forth—constricts the aura even more, thus increasing its vulnerability.

Further enfeebling the constricted aura are small clusters of darkness, a feature commonly found in the auras of psychic vampires. These dark clusters are like parasites that attach themselves to the constricted aura system and feed upon it—a condition that comes close to parasitic vampirism, which we will discuss in a later chapter. While the origins of dark clusters are in dispute, they are believed to involve rejection, abuse, traumatic events, and possibly a history of vampire victimization, each of which also tends to constrict the aura, particularly when they occur early in life.

A grayish discoloration is another characteristic often found throughout the constricted aura. Persons with this feature are often pessimistic, insecure, and distrustful. When we add discoloration to the constricted, dark clustered aura, we have a tragic three-ingredient formula for even greater vulnerability to psychic vampirism.

Aura Liberation Procedure

The Aura Liberation Procedure is designed to energize the constricted aura while replacing discoloration and clusters of darkness with an abundant supply of luminous energy. This procedure is likewise effective in dissolving dark fragments associated with the aura vampire virus as discussed earlier in this chapter. As a growth-related, self-energizing procedure, the procedure exercises the aura's inner core, unblocks clogged energy channels, and illuminates the total aura with bright, abundant energy. The end result is a renewed, attuned aura with power to resist any external threat of vampirism. Equally as important, this procedure, once mastered, can effectively banish any tendency, regardless of its severity, toward psychic vampirism within the self. These results can be fortified by other procedures designed specifically to protect and energize the aura.

This procedure is uniquely different from most aura empowerment approaches in that it introduces intuitive aura perception, a strategy involving clairvoyance in which the full aura is perceived psychically.

Step 1. Preliminary Aura Viewing. Begin the procedure by using the Aura Hand-viewing Procedure as previously presented to view your aura as seen around your hand and lower arm.

Step 2. Intuitive Aura Perception. Once the aura is visible, use your intuitive powers to view your full aura by first reminding yourself that the aura enveloping your hand and lower arm is representative of your total aura. Then with your eyes closed, trust your intuitive powers to reveal your full aura with its variety of characteristics—coloration, clusters, fissures, streamers, expansiveness, and so forth. Take all the time you need for your aura to become clearly visible in your mind. Remind yourself that your aura is highly receptive to your intuitive mind. Identify any problem areas or deficiencies anywhere in your aura system, including damage to the aura resulting from a psychic vampire attack. This step may require some practice, but you will find it increasingly easy to intuitively view your aura.

Step 3. Relaxation. Having intuitively viewed your full aura, settle back, and give yourself permission to become fully relaxed by mentally scanning your body from your forehead downward, releasing all tension as you go. As relaxation slowly spreads throughout your body, let your breathing become deep and rhythmic. Imagine yourself breathing in the bright energies of peaceful relaxation and exhaling the dark refuse of anxiety and stress. Let all your worries take flight, like balloons drifting far away in a gentle breeze until they are finally out of sight. Think of time as slowing down as you continue to breathe deeply and rhythmically.

Step 4. Intuitive Aura Perception. As in Step 1, again visualize your full aura as an extension of the aura around your hand and lower arm. As before, note your aura's existing boundaries and structural characteristics, to include any area of weakness, darkness, or discoloration.

Step 5. Aura Exercise. Shift your attention again to your breathing. While continuing to breathe deeply and rhythmically, give yourself permission to exercise your aura by expanding it as you inhale and contracting it as you exhale. Note the energizing effect of the rhythmic expanding/contracting process as it washes away any remaining dullness from your aura, leaving behind only bright energy. Sense dark clusters slowly dissolving and voids becoming infused with bright, new energy. As you rhythmically inhale and exhale, let the core of your aura pulsate rhythmically with your breathing, fully energizing and attuning your aura while expanding it to its outer limits.

Step 6. Post-intervention Aura Viewing. Again, use the Aura Hand-viewing Strategy to view your aura. Note its fresh brilliance and increased expansiveness.

Step 7. Aura Energizing Cue. You can at any time expand, attune, and energize your full aura by simply taking in a deep breath and exhaling slowly as you sense yourself inhaling the bright energies of peaceful relaxation and exhaling the dark residue of anxiety and stress. Affirm your power to use this convenient cue as needed to activate the effects of the full procedure.

In our efforts to evaluate the effectiveness of the Aura Liberation Procedure, we obtained electrophotographs of the right index fingertip before and after the procedure for ten participating subjects. Without exception, dramatic differences were noted in the pairs of photographs. As illustrated in Figure 6 (shown below), the procedure not only increased brightness in the aura, it expanded the aura as well. As the aura increased in brilliance and expansiveness, areas of discoloration vanished and grayish clusters took on a fresh new brightness. Before and after viewings of the full aura by trained aura specialists revealed similar effects throughout the full aura. These changes in the visible aura suggest a revitalized, fully functional inner aura core with power to generate abundant anti-vampire energy and disperse it throughout the full aura system.

The Aura Self-protection Massage

A highly effective strategy for energizing and protecting the aura system against psychic vampirism is the Aura Self-protection Massage. This self-administered strategy exercises the total aura system and

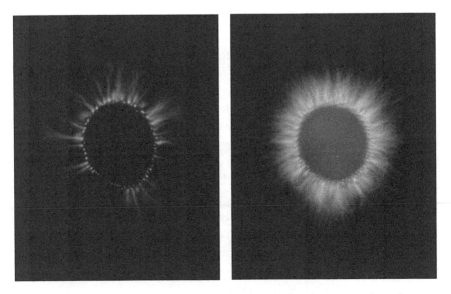

FIGURE 6. THE AURA LIBERATION PROCEDURE, BEFORE (LEFT) AND AFTER (RIGHT).

activates its internal defense powers. It is especially effective in attuning and balancing the aura. While several aura massage strategies require an experienced aura massage specialist, the Aura Self-protection Massage is easily self-administered. It requires no previous practice or experience using aura massage techniques.

The Aura Self-protection Massage is based on the simple premise that interventions involving a localized but critical area of the aura can affect the full aura. Just as a vampire attack to a specific region of the aura can affect the total aura, certain aura massage procedures that target a specific aura region can energize and empower the total aura. The Aura Self-protection Massage uses clockwise and counterclockwise massage techniques designed to exercise and jump-start the aura's inner core situated in the body's solar plexus region. By focusing on the aura's innermost core, the procedure not only raises the aura's overall energy level, it generates a frequency pattern that effectively repels psychic vampirism in whatever its form. Throughout the procedure, only the enveloping aura is massaged—any physical contact with the body can interrupt the empowering effects of the massage. Here is the procedure.

Step 1. Clockwise Massage. While in a relaxed, seated, or reclining position, with your hands resting comfortably at your sides, take a few moments to visualize the aura enveloping your physical body and the bright, energizing aura core situated in your solar plexus. Place your right hand, palm side down, a few inches above your solar plexus, and begin to massage your aura at that region with small, circular, clockwise movements. Gradually expand the circular aura massage to encompass a larger body region surrounding your solar plexus. Sense the energy swirling in a clockwise direction, first around your solar plexus, then expanding to include your chest and lower abdomen. Following a few moments of clockwise massage, rest your hand to your side as you continue to experience the swirling energy throughout your central body region.

Step 2. Counterclockwise Massage. With your right hand now resting comfortably at your side, place your left hand, palm side down, a few inches above your solar plexus and reverse the clockwise massage to induce counterclockwise motion in the aura. Begin the massage at that region with small, circular, counterclockwise movements. As with the clockwise massage, gradually expand the counterclockwise massage to encompass a larger body region surrounding your solar plexus. Sense the energy swirling in a counterclockwise direction, first around your solar plexus, then expanding to include your chest and lower abdomen. Following a few moments of counterclockwise massage, rest your left hand to your side as you continue to experience the swirling energy throughout your central body region.

Step 3. Repeat Massage. Further exercise the aura system by repeating Steps 1 and 2 above. Throughout the massage, think of your aura's inner core as a powerful generator of energy. Notice the energy building in your central aura region and then spreading throughout your total aura system to envelop your body with a powerful shield of bright new energy.

Step 4. Balancing and Attuning. To balance and attune the aura's new energies, close your eyes and touch your temples with the fingertips of both hands as you sense vibrant energy permeating your total being.

Step 5. Energizing Affirmation. Affirm in your own words the empowering effects of this exercise. Examples are: *I am fully energized and empowered. The innermost part of my being is now balanced and attuned. I am enveloped in a powerful shield of energy. I am protected and secure.*

Step 6. Energizing Cue. Affirm in your own words your ability to instantly activate the empowering effects of the full procedure by simply closing your eyes and touching your temples with your fingertips as you envision a bright outer shield of energy enveloping your total aura.

As with other aura empowerment procedures, the effects of the Aura Self-protection Massage can be seen by viewing the aura using the Aura Hand-viewing Procedure immediately before and after the massage. Invariably, the massage expands the aura and increases its brilliance. When the procedure is practiced daily, colors in the aura become more vivid and such enfeebling structural features as breaks and voids soon disappear.

Aside from protecting the aura, the Aura Self-protection Massage is highly useful in repairing damage to the aura inflicted by a psychic vampire attack. The puncture wound and accompanying discoloration in the aura are particularly receptive to this corrective strategy. Even when the specific location of damage to the aura is unknown, the procedure tends to infuse the damaged area with healing energy and replace the surrounding discoloration with bright new energy.

The procedure's energizing cue (Step 6) of simply touching the forehead combined with appropriate imagery is both convenient and effective. After sufficient practice using the full procedure, the easy cue alone can protect and energize the aura. In stressful or threatening situations, it can instantly generate a state of security and well-being.

Finger Interlock Procedure

The Finger Interlock Procedure is one the most popular and extensively research strategies known for protecting the human energy system. It erects a powerful outer shield of radiant energy, commonly called the *halo effect* around the full aura. The halo effect protects the aura against the onslaught of psychic vampirism or any other intrusive force. Aside from protecting the aura system, this multifunctional procedure serves at least three other functions. First, it generates balance within the self's energy system while attuning it to the highest cosmic source of energy; second, it produces a state of relaxation and well-being; and third, it builds motivation and promotes success in achieving a wide range of personal goals. For evaluation purposes, aura viewings are included as options at the beginning and end of the procedure (Steps 1 and 7). These optional steps are not critical to the effectiveness of the procedure.

Step 1 (Optional). Preliminary Aura Viewing. Using the Aura Hand-viewing Procedure, view the aura, noting any signs of constriction or weakness.

Step 2. Cognitive Relaxation. Find a comfortable place and take a few moments to mentally relax your body, beginning with the muscles in your forehead and slowly progressing downward. As you scan your body downward, let every fiber and tendon become loose and limp. Envision the tension leaving your body as a mist slowly rising and then vanishing.

Step 3. Finger Interlock. Bring together the thumb and middle finger of each hand to form two circles, then join your hands to form interlocking circles.

Step 4. Affirmation. Hold the finger interlock position as you affirm: *I am totally enveloped with powerful energy. I am balanced within and fully attuned to the higher cosmos. I am protected, secure, and shielded from all harm.*

Step 5. Cosmic Infusion. Relax your hands, and with your palms turned upward, envision bright rays of pure energy from the highest cosmos entering your palms and infusing your total being. Affirm: *I am at one with the cosmos. All the power of the universe in now available to me.* Specify your personal goals and affirm your success in achieving them.

Step 6. Finger Interlock Cue. In your own words, affirm that by simply forming the finger interlock as a cue, you can instantly activate the empowerment effects of the full procedure at any time.

Step 7 (Optional). Post-intervention Aura Viewing. Again, view your aura using the Aura Hand-viewing Procedure. Note the changes in the aura, particularly its increased brightness and expansiveness. With practice, you will detect the halo effect, a bright sphere of energy enveloping and protecting the aura system.

Electrophotographs of the right index fingertip obtained before and after this procedure almost always revealed the halo effect following the procedure, a temporary but impenetrable armor which is one of our best protections against any impending threat of psychic vampirism. You can view the halo effect when it is present in the aura of others through such viewing strategies as the Peripheral Gaze Procedure.

This Finger Interlock Procedure is easily mastered and one of the most powerful strategies available for protecting the aura against a psychic vampire attack, or once an attack is underway, to instantly terminate it. Everyone, including mental health professionals who often work with patients prone to psychic vampirism, can benefit from the protection provide by this procedure and the inconspicuous finger interlock cue, which requires only seconds to implement. I use the cue regularly and make it a practice to teach the full procedure to my patients and students as an invaluable empowerment strategy (see Figure 7, following page).

Although designed primarily to combat psychic vampirism, the Finger Interlock Procedure is an excellent strategy for various other personal empowerment goals, such as improving memory and concentration, reducing stress, overcoming fear, and building self-esteem. Having mastered the strategy, you can use the convenient finger interlock cue at almost any time or place to instantly activate any of the procedure's many functions. College students enrolled in my courses have used the cue to overcome stage fright, improve test performance, and accelerate learning of complex skills. As with some of the other empowerment cues we have discussed, you can use the finger interlock before or during important examinations, job interviews, and public presentations, to mention but a few of the wide-ranging possibilities.

The simple cue is so inconspicuous and easily executed that it has become popular among performing artists, actors, politicians, ministers, TV reporters, and other public figures. Many professional athletes are known to use the cue before and during competitive events to improve the quality of their performance. They believe the cue unleashes a reserve of energy that increases endurance and improves concentration, coordination, and accuracy in a variety of sports activities.

Cosmic Connection Procedure

Our efforts to energize and empower the aura are always enriched by a recognition of our cosmic origins and awareness of higher cosmic sources of power. Strategies that attune the aura system to the cosmos can effectively balance its functions while literally connecting it to an unlimited reserve of cosmic power. When the aura is balanced, attuned, and connected to the cosmos, it automatically repels any threat of psychic vampirism. The Cosmic Connection Procedure recognizes our capacity to achieve that important goal. It is built on the premise that the mind, body, and spirit are in constant interaction, both within the self and with the higher cosmos. The procedure is designed to guide that interaction in ways that generate a balanced

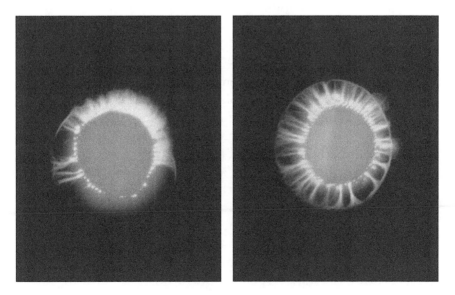

FIGURE 7. THE HALO EFFECT BEFORE (LEFT) AND AFTER (RIGHT)
THE FINGER INTERLOCK PROCEDURE.

and attuned state of full empowerment—mentally, physically, and spiritually.

This procedure introduces the concept of mind-over-aura intervention, a form of psychokinesis, or PK, that recognizes the power of the mind to influence the physical body and its aura energy system. Here is the procedure.

> **Step 1. Preliminary Aura Viewing.** Find a quiet, comfortable place and, using the Aura Hand-viewing Procedure previously discussed, view your own aura, paying particular attention to the aura's expansiveness, coloration, and specific structural characteristics.

> **Step 2. Sensory Awareness.** Close your eyes and note your body's various physical sensations. Listen to the messages of your body. Note any tightness of muscles, areas of discomfort, and fatigue, each of which is an important cue that suggests constriction or imbalance in the aura. Sense areas of possible damage to the aura, including any localized area of dull pain or numbness. An area of dull pain is often a residual effect of a vampire attack that either punctured or lacerated the aura; whereas numbness is associated with vampire encounters that drained energy from the aura by interfacing it but without inflicting structural damage.

> **Step 3. Mind-over-aura Intervention.** Visualize the aura's energy core situated in your solar plexus and sense its energies flowing throughout your body and surrounding aura. Focus your attention on specific areas of aura weakness or damage, and mentally bathe them with abundant energy. Visualize discoloration or darkness in the aura slowly dissolving, leaving behind only brightness. Let the energy flowing outward from your aura's powerful core saturate every affected area, infusing it with bright healing energy. Visualize bright energy filling in voids, closing fissures, and mending puncture wounds. Visualize bright streams of energy as luminous threads suturing the aura's open wounds while fully infusing the aura with healing energy. Stay with each dysfunctional area until it is totally energized.

Step 4. Cosmic Infusion. Visualize the distant, luminous core of cosmos dispersing bountiful energy in its purest form throughout the universe. Give your own energy system permission to be fully bathed in bright cosmic energy. Sense the balancing of your own energy system as it melds with the cosmic source of boundless energy. Let your own energy system become fully energized and attuned to that highest cosmic dimension of power.

Step 5. Affirmation. Bring together your hands and connect your fingertips as a symbol of balance as you affirm in your own words the procedure's energizing, empowering effects. Examples are: *Every fiber of my being is now fully energized. I am balanced and attuned to the highest cosmic source of life and energy. I am protected and empowered.*

Step 6. Post-intervention Aura Viewing. Once again, view your aura using the Aura Hand-viewing Procedure. Note the changes in your aura, to include such features as brightness, expansiveness, and symmetry.

Step 7. Aura Empowerment Cue. To reactivate the empowering effects of this procedure at any time, simply bring together your hands and connect your fingertips as you visualize sparkling energy radiating from your aura's inner core melding with bright rays of pure energy radiating from the greater cosmic core. Sense the wondrous infusion of radiant energy throughout your total being.

As with other aura empowerment procedures, the Cosmic Connection Procedure generates a highly energized state that is readily visible in the aura. Self-viewings of the aura as well as viewings by trained aura specialists revealed striking changes in the aura's brightness and expansiveness, observations that were confirmed by electrophotographic recordings obtained before and after the procedure as illustrated in Figure 8 (see following page).

Cosmic Color Procedure

We are at our peak of power when our energy system is fully infused with cosmic energy. The Cosmic Color Procedure is designed to energize the full aura while directly applying concentrated masses of colorful cosmic energy to specific areas of vulnerability. The procedure is based on our laboratory studies concerning the phenomenal power of color imagery. Amazing as it may seem, our studies found that simply envisioning a particular color can introduce that color into the aura system, while at the same time activating the empowerment potential related to it. For instance, imagery of luminous green can literally introduce healing and rejuvenating energy into the aura. Equally as amazing, by envisioning bright yellow, we can actually sharpen our intellect while enriching our social relationships. Our studies found that envisioning bright purple or violet was often accompanied by either spiritual enlightenment of increased awareness of a spirit guide.

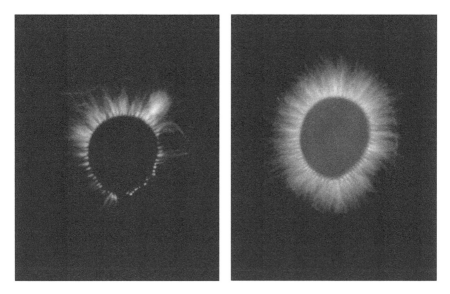

FIGURE 8. COSMIC CONNECTION PROCEDURE, BEFORE (LEFT) AND AFTER (RIGHT).

Our discovery of the effects of color imagery on the aura system gave inspiration for a series of follow-up studies concerning the relevance of the color found in the higher cosmic realm. Using a variety of techniques, including interactions with discarnates and out-of-body travel to the cosmic realm, our studies found that the cosmic dimension—not unlike the human aura—consists of a brilliant core of pure white energy and expansive planes of various colors. By paralleling the design of the higher cosmos, the human aura with its bright core and radiating colors provides a striking manifestation of our cosmic origin.

Equally as striking as the parallel in designs of the aura and the higher cosmos are similarities in the empowerment significance of particular colors, whether found in the aura or the higher cosmos. Our studies further discovered that the effects of a particular color image can be augmented by imagery of the cosmic plane of that same color. The effects of color imagery can be increased even further when the selected color is actually massaged into the aura. As might be expected, the empowerment effects of color strategies reached their peaks when the procedure included astral travel to designated cosmic planes of color, which we will discuss in a later chapter.

Through the Cosmic Color Procedure, we can identify weak or vulnerable areas of the aura and infuse them with relevant cosmic color energy. Areas of damage and malfunction resulting from psychic vampire attacks are particular responsive to this procedure. Routine practice of the procedure generates a healthy, balanced aura system with vampire defense resources sufficient to repel any threat of psychic vampirism. Here is the procedure.

Step 1. Goal Statement. While resting comfortably, formulate your empowerment goals, and affirm your intent to achieve them.

Step 2. Cosmic Imagery. With your eyes closed, visualize the cosmic realm as a dimension of wondrous beauty. Visualize the center of the cosmos as a bright region of light around which are arranged many planes of color. Take plenty of time for images to spontaneously unfold. At this critical step, you may experience the presence of a special cosmic entity gently guiding the imagery process. Remind yourself that you can rely on images that are guided by the magnanimous cosmic force. Think of the cosmic realm as an ever-present reality rather than some distant, detached dimension with little relevance to your present existence.

Step 3. Cosmic Interface. Turn your palms upward as you sense the merging of your aura with the cosmic dimension. With the interfacing of the two systems—the one within yourself and the other in the higher cosmos—you are now empowered to access the energy resources of specialized cosmic planes.

Step 4. Specialized Infusion. With your eyes closed, visualize the wide range of colorful cosmic planes, and identify the plane that meets your most pressing empowerment need and center your full attention on that plane. For psychic protection, as well as for health and rejuvenation, focus on the luminous green plane; for cognitive enrichment, focus on the bright yellow plane; for spiritual resources, focus on the violet or purple plane; for peaceful tranquillity, focus on the bright blue plane. Use your intuitive insight to select other appropriate planes. Almost always, the plane that stands out in brightness or expansiveness is usually pertinent to your aura's present energy needs.

Step 5. Energy Melding. Upon selecting the appropriate plane, gently rub your palms together as you sense the energies of the plane you selected melding with the energies of your aura. Sense the orb of colorful energy building between your palms.

Optional Step. Cosmic Viewing. You can view the colorful orb of energy between your palms by using a variation of the Aura Hand-viewing Procedure as follows: First hold your hands at arms length with palm facing palm; then with your palms cupped, gaze at the space between them. Slowly expand your peripheral vision and let your eyes fall slightly out of focus.

You will then notice a white glow between your palms. Finally, gaze at the glow until color appears, typically within a few seconds. With practice using this strategy, you will find the energy orb formed between your palms to be the same in color as that of the cosmic plane you selected in Step 2 above.

Step 6. Energy Massage. Place the orb of cosmic energy over your solar plexus and, with your palms turned toward your body, gently massage the new energy into your aura using any variation of slow, circular movements while carefully avoiding physical touch. Conclude the massage with slow, vertical movements over your central body region.

Step 7. Specialized Massage. To massage a specific aura region or particular body area, repeat Steps 4 and 5 above to gather another energy sphere of appropriate cosmic color, and massage it into the aura at the affected location, to include any damaged aura or dysfunctional body region. For empowerment of a particular body organ, massage the orb of cosmic energy into the aura at the location of that organ.

Step 8. Affirmation and Empowerment Cue. With your eyes closed, again envision the cosmic plane from which the sphere of energy was taken. Restate the empowerment goals you formulated at the beginning of this procedure, and in your own words affirm them as not simply goals but unfolding realities. Affirm that by simply visualizing the cosmos with its bright core and multiple planes of colorful energy, you can instantly activate the empowerment effects of this procedure.

Steps 1 and 2 are especially critical to the success of the Cosmic Infusion Procedure. Even in the absence of the remaining steps, these two steps can be a profound source of insight and power. A wondrous awareness of the cosmos and the vastness of its resources can empower us to face life's most difficult challenges with unlimited confidence and peace.

In researching this procedure, we discovered that the Specialized Massage (Step 7) has almost unlimited personal empowerment possibilities. That finding is consistent with the view that the cosmic realm consists not only of its bright cosmic core of energy in its purest form, but also of numerous specialized cosmic planes, each with different empowerment potentials based on the coloration of the plane's energy. As noted in the procedure, planes of luminous green are related to mental and physical health; planes of bright yellow are related intellectual efficiency; and planes of violet or purple are related to spiritual insight, to mention but a few of the many color options and their related empowerment possibilities.

Our search for effective pain management options found that green luminous energy, once massaged directly into the aura at the area of pain, reduced the intensity of pain, often replacing it with sensations of either warmth or, according to the descriptions of many patients, a wooden-like feeling. While further research is needed, the luminous green massage has also shown promise in its capacity to accelerate healing.

The Cosmic Color Procedure has been especially useful in facilitating various intellectual functions. For that application, the procedure accesses energy at Step 5 from the bright yellow plane and massages it into the aura at the head region. As improbable as it may seem, marked improvements on objective measurements of problem solving, memory, and comprehension were noted following a single application of this procedure. Along another line, the localized aura massage has been extremely effective as an aphrodisiac when rich gold cosmic energy is massaged into the aura at the genital region. The procedure has been especially useful in the treatment of sexual arousal disorders, particularly male erectile problems.

For spiritual goals—including heightened awareness of spiritual guides and discarnate beings—a period of quietness following the procedure is recommended. During that meditative state, a spiritual presence commonly manifests itself, often with highly relevant messages.

Taken together, the evidence is clear. Deliberate, step-by-step intervention into the aura's functions can profoundly influence the aura while promoting a state of full personal empowerment—mentally, physically, and spiritually.

Summary

In this chapter, we explored the nature of the human aura and examined its relevance to psychic vampirism. We examined the significance of the aura's various structural and color characteristics. We developed ways of viewing and interpreting the aura; and finally, we presented ways of empowering the aura and using aura energy as a resource to promote our personal growth.

Critical to our search for personal empowerment is better understanding the human aura system, not simply as an external energy phenomenon, but as an integral component of our total being. By understanding the aura and mastering the procedures related to it, we can better use its power not only to cope with psychic vampirism, but also to enrich the quality of our lives.

It is important to note that the aura empowerment procedures presented in this chapter are not etched in stone. Like other procedures presented throughout this book, they are flexible and can be readily adapted to meet variations in personal preferences and needs. Specific components can be modified or practiced independently of the full procedure; or they can be combined with components of other strategies to form a totally new approach tailored to fit us individually. For instance, the aura circular massage can be used in conjunction with mind-over-body intervention techniques to repair a fissure in the aura or close a puncture wound inflicted by a psychic vampire attack. Only through practice can we discover the strategies, or combination of strategies, that work best for us individually.

Our mental, physical, and spiritual empowerment rests largely on knowledge and skills related to the human aura.

FIVE

Group Psychic Vampirism

GROUP PSYCHIC VAMPIRISM is an extremely common phenomenon that can occur wherever groups gather, and in some instances, throughout the world at large as we will later see. In contrast to one-on-one psychic vampirism, which is an energy encounter between one psychic vampire and one host victim, group psychic vampirism can involve multiple vampires and multiple victims. More specifically, it can take any of the following forms: (1) encounters between one psychic vampire and multiple host victims; (2) encounters between multiple psychic vampires and one host victim; and (3) encounters between multiple psychic vampires and multiple host victims.

As energized beings, we routinely interact with others, not only in sending and receiving energy, but also in generating new energy through the interactive process. The total amount of energy produced by the social interaction is often greater than the sum of the energies contributed independently by each participant, an effect known as synergistic. Typically, the greater the number of persons participating in a positive, productive interaction, the greater the synergistic effect. The results can be an enriched energy infusion for all participants as well as an accumulation of peripheral energy that can reach far beyond the group. Political and inspirational events in particular are often deliberately planned to generate a sweeping synergistic effect that reaches far beyond the immediate group.

The synergistic effect resulting from the collective efforts of groups has been dramatically illustrated in laboratory experiments involving psychokinesis (PK). PK is the human capacity—individually or in groups—to mentally influence objects, events, and processes in the absence of physical or instrumental intervention. In a very early research effort designed to investigate the collective power of PK at Athens State University, we devised an experimental situation in which a pendulum was suspended under a bell jar on a table, with two groups of 22 subjects each situated at opposite sides of the pendulum. The two groups were instructed to mentally bring the pendulum into motion through their energized pushing and pulling efforts. A metronome was used to pace the two group's efforts—as one group mentally pushed against the pendulum, the other group mentally pulled the pendulum toward them. A series of five-minute "push-pull" sessions was provided with a brief rest period following each session. On the third session, the pendulum showed first a turning motion, and then a distinct swinging movement. The metronome was then stopped, and the two groups successfully accelerated the movement of the pendulum until it struck the sides of the bell jar. Equally as significant, the groups then brought the pendulum to a rapid stop by simply reversing their push-pull efforts. The experiment was replicated several times, and each time the results were the same, thus suggesting a remarkable synergistic capacity of our collective mental resources to directly influence conditions and induce change, whether for better or worse. Unfortunately, in collective psychic vampirism, the synergistic effect is detrimental and in some instances severely damaging to others.

In my seminars, I often promote a synergistic interaction designed to energize and empower not only the group, but the planet as well. Empowering energy is flawless—it is constructive energy that, once unleashed, knows no bounds. It can travel at cosmic speeds. It can be focused on specific targets at hand or it can be dispersed to envelop the globe. Beyond that, it can probe the farthest reaches of the universe. We will later present group strategies that are designed to generate and disperse empowering energy.

In contrast to empowering energy, disempowering energy is always constrictive. Its effects, however, vary depending on the nature of the group. In certain instances, the negative energy generated by groups is extremely destructive. Examples are the destructive energies generated by hate groups that practice such vampire tactics as bigotry, prejudice, intolerance, racism, and exclusion. Like parasites, they soon exhaust the limited energy resources within the group, and then turn to dangerous acting-out that too often includes violence, all in a futile effort to advance and recharge the group. Their strategies can include various degrees of openly antisocial and hostile behavior designed to intimidate, harass, and control. The unfortunate consequences for group participants are arrested growth and a distortion of the normal functions of the internal energy system. While the deviant group may temporarily thrive on the destructive energy it generates, it eventually self-destructs.

Group psychic vampirism can occur within groups as well as between groups. It can involve opposing groups in which one group organizes its energies and other resources to subdue and defeat another group. In highly competitive situations, psychic vampire tactics can be subtly disguised to manipulate, confuse, and divide the opposition. In heated political campaigns, for instance, vampire-like tactics designed to de-energize and defeat the opposition are common. Similarly, vampire-like tactics are often observed in competitive sports situations, particularly in the final minutes of highly competitive contests where its effects, if not countered, can be decisive in determining the winner. Psychic vampirism in competitive team sports, however, is usually seen as justifiable vampirism since the goal of both teams is to defeat the opposition rather than to inflict harm. Furthermore, competitive vampirism is typically spontaneous and, in many instances, inherent in the nature of the sport. It can include strategies designed to intimidate the opposition, interrupt its coordination, deplete its energy, and exhaust its team spirit.

Competitive sports teams that are energized early in an event but have difficulty staying energized may be victims of psychic vampirism rather than game-induced fatigue. The vampire source of fatigue may be the opposing team as well as opposing spectators. Supportive, energized, wildly cheering spectators not only raise the expectations and energy level of their preferred team; they lower the expectations and energy level of the opposition. Obviously, the larger and more energized the supportive spectator group, the more effective their vampire efforts.

In my practice, I frequently work with sports teams to build their success expectancies as well as their vampire resistance powers. Whether for soccer, football, basketball, or baseball, my approach includes strategies that infuse the team with abundant energy while increasing resistance to group psychic vampirism. Even scholars bowl and debate teams have benefited from strategies designed to stimulate concentration and combat the disconcerting effects of psychic vampirism. The teams are provided with empowerment cues, including images or gestures, which can be used intermittently throughout the competitive event. Later, we will present detailed, energizing procedures that can be used by groups to repel psychic vampirism.

Along another line, group psychic vampirism is particularly common in the work setting where it can influence employee performance and relationships at all levels within an organization. As in person-to-person vampirism, the immediate results are a new supply of energy for the psychic vampire, and low energy for the unfortunate host victims. This was illustrated by an assistant business manager who, in therapy, presented fatigue and low-back pain, which she attributed to job stress. Analysis of her work situation revealed, however, that her symptoms were more noticeable when she worked closely with a particular team. When working independently of the team, her energy level returned to normal and the pain ceased. Suspecting group vampirism, I prescribed a vampire protection strategy applicable to her work situation. Freshly energized and free of pain, she took command of the work situation that had for months drained her of energy. Almost immediately, her job became more satisfying, and she soon reached a totally new level of job satisfaction and personal fulfillment.

Aside from a variety of physical symptoms, psychic vampirism in the work setting can have other very serious consequences. Almost always, vampirized victims become increasingly dissatisfied with their jobs, and the quality of their performance declines. Among other major signs of vampire victimization among employees in the workplace are high accident rates, low morale, excessive absenteeism, and high employee turnover. Since psychic vampires typically select target victims within a reasonable striking range, analysis of relevant job-related data can identify localized work areas or departments that are especially prone to psychic vampirism.

Group psychic vampirism can, unfortunately, occur in the family setting where the psychic vampire systematically consumes the energies of other family members. Psychic vampires in the family situation are almost always discontent and resentful. They tend to be critical of other family members, and they often complain of being misunderstood. They are often emotionally cold and distant. Many of them experience smoldering hostility and alienation from the family. They feel unappreciated and insecure, and they tend to blame others—including other family members—for their problems and failures. They are usually irritable, impatient, and highly temperamental.

Certain gender differences have been noted among psychic vampires in the family situation. The female vampire tends to be manipulative and passively controlling, whereas the male vampire is more likely to be assertive and defiant. In their interactions within the family as well as with people in general, both male and female vampires tend to be emotionally distant and superficially independent, but underneath they feel insecure and vulnerable.

In working with families where psychic vampirism is suspected, I often use role-playing in which all immediate family members are present. Family interactions are first observed, and then the family member who demonstrates vampire traits is assigned the role of a supportive, nurturing, and caring person. To keep the focus on the family rather than the suspected vampire only, other family members are assigned roles that emphasize positive interactions and acceptance of others.

In family role-playing, persons with psychic vampire traits are instructed to practice praise, patience, acceptance, and understanding. Although they may at first experience difficulty assuming the non-vampire role, they soon discover its positive, energizing effects on both themselves and others. Although not instructed to be emotionally expressive in their assigned roles, most of them become increasingly responsive toward other family members as role-playing progresses. Each role-playing session is usually concluded with a group exercise that focus on harmonious family interactions as well as inner attunement and balance.

Always, the most effective treatment approach for persons or groups with psychic vampire traits centers on potentials rather than problems and solutions rather than diagnostic labels.

Vampire Surfing and Infiltration

In group psychic vampire situations, the amount of energy lost by host victims can range from barely noticeable to extremely profound. Some experienced psychic vampires are known to survey the group and draw small measures of energy from large numbers of persons making up the group. This practice, which we call *vampire surfing,* often takes place at large public gatherings, such as concerts, conferences, lectures, and conventions. Like surfing the Internet, they go from source to source, pausing only briefly for minimal input. The input in vampire surfing, of course, is energy rather than information.

Host victims of vampire surfing seldom notice the energy loss except when their energy system is already stressed or deficient in some way. If, however, vampire surfing is sufficiently extensive, the audience will eventually become listless, drowsy, and fatigued. This could help explain why many events begin on an enthusiastically high note, only to end at a disappointingly low key. Even in highly energized events, such as rock concerts and political conventions, vampire surfing is widespread and can exact a heavy toll. When the audience is large, vampire surfers typically prefer a seating situation, such as a balcony or skybox, which provides an overview of the group being vampirized.

Vampire surfing, like other forms of group vampirism, can occur wherever people gather—auditoriums, theaters, churches, stadiums, classrooms, and so forth. Vampire surfers are often skilled psychic vampires who are quite socially active. Surfing for them is more than energizing, it is amusing and challenging as well. They often engage in multiple social activities—including professional, political, educational, theatrical, and religious—for the express purpose of surfing. They thrive on publicity and public recognition of their achievements and contributions to the community. They often hold membership in numerous civic and professional organizations. Although their energies are often quite scattered, they are usually good organizers who volunteer to spearhead important projects and civic events. They are outgoing and vivacious, but not always financially successful because of imprudent investments and unsound business deals. Their mood state is usually elevated, except when their energy reaches a critical low level, whereupon they seek an "energizing social situation" or a new social cause to exercise their vampire drive and increase their energy supply.

While acutely aware of their need for social involvement, vampire surfers often deny the vampire nature of their social interactions. Many surfers, however, are keenly aware of the vampire drive and readily admit extracting energy intentionally from others through their vampire excursions. Here is the report of a vampire surfer who, as a funeral director, believed his vampire interactions were like a sedative that generated a calming effect on a grieving audience:

I would not label myself a psychic vampire, but I admit that I am energized by being around groups, especially at funerals. In my profession, I direct several funerals each week, sometimes two or three a day. From my background position as director during the funeral ceremony, I often find myself scanning the audience and spontaneously taking in the enormous overflow of emotional energy that funerals seem to generate. As a result, the intensity of the occasion usually subsides and mourners seem to become calm and more at ease. I, on the other hand, become exhilarated and at times overwhelmed by the intake of energy spilling over from the audience.

In vampire surfing, the minuscule amount of energy drawn from each individual is usually below that level required to be noticeable, a threshold sometimes called the *just noticeable difference* (JND). My interviews with experienced vampire surfers revealed that during surfing they are usually sensitive to cues suggesting the JND threshold is about to be reached. They reported that when a host group appeared tired or drowsy, the JND threshold was near at hand. According to vampire surfers, a slumped posture and downward gaze are sure signals that the JND threshold is imminent. When vampire surfing is extensive, an entire audience can show these symptoms. But even victims who are familiar with the concept of group psychic vampirism may not associate their symptoms with vampire surfing, since the energy loss is below their threshold for conscious awareness. Consequently, experienced psychic vampires typically surf incognito and with impunity—they are at once energized and unnoticed.

While vampire surfers typically draw small amounts of energy from large numbers of persons, they are also known to survey groups expressly to identify particularly vulnerable prey. The host victims they select may range from naive group leaders to passive members of the audience. Their victims usually lack insight into psychic vampirism, and they are usually bereft of psychic coping and protection resources—deficiencies that make them nonresistant.

Although vampire surfing is usually initiated by a single individual, it can be an organized, collective activity in which a vampire subgroup strategically positioned within a gathering extracts substantial energy from the larger group, a sophisticated phenomenon we call *vampire infiltration*. The goal of vampire infiltration is to exhaust, divide, or scatter the larger group's energy through subtle strategies rather than through active confrontation that can intensify the larger group's resistance. Gatherings involving controversial issues such as the environment, trade policies, and human rights are particularly vulnerable to vampire infiltration. Political events are often targets of vampire infiltration. From town meetings to national conventions, vampire infiltration, unless counteracted, can de-energize a group and markedly reduce its effectiveness. Fortunately, group procedures are now available to guard against both vampire surfing and vampire infiltration.

Group Empowerment Procedure

The Group Empowerment Procedure is designed for use by groups to (1) efficiently organize their existing energy resources, (2) infuse the group with new energy, and (3) protect the group from the invasion of psychic vampirism and other enfeebling influences. Aside from exercising the group's energy resources, the procedure recognizes the significance of the group's expectations and commitment, each of which has important energizing potentials. Equally as important, it recognizes the synergistic effect of group participation. Once each member of the group is energized, the total group is enveloped in a protective aura of powerful energy. The procedure effectively repels vampire surfing and infiltration as previously discussed. When the procedure is practiced by the group, active psychic vampires often leave the group immediately following the procedure, if not at some point during the procedure.

The procedure is flexible and can be adapted to the makeup and needs of almost any group. Because of its energizing and motivational effects, it is especially recommended for use at the beginning of a group event. It is also effective as a closing group exercise. The procedure is practiced step-by-step by the full group. Here is the procedure.

Step 1. Group Interfacing. Together with the group, stand and with the palms of your hands turned outward, briefly interface—but without touching—the palms of surrounding persons one-by-one while sensing the merging of energies in your palms. Think of your palms as sending and receiving antennae for your internal energy system.

Step 2. Cosmic Interfacing. While seated and with your eyes closed, join the group in turning the palms of your hands upward in recognition of the cosmic source of all energy. Together with the group, sense the powerful merging of cosmic energy with the energies in your palms. As the cosmic energy system remains interfaced with your own, allow a few moments for the energizing process to continue until your total being is infused and overflowing with powerful energy.

Step 3. Group Energy Infusion. Together with the group, turn the palms of your hands outward and while moving them side-to-side, allow the new infusion of abundant energy to spill over to envelop the total group with a bright, impenetrable aura of energy. You, along with the total group, are now fully energized and protected.

Step 4. Group Reflection. Together with the group, quietly reflect on relevant personal as well as group goals, and commit your energies to achieving them.

Step 5. Conclusion. Balance and attune your energy system by bringing your hands together—palm against palm—as you affirm in unison with the group: *As a group, we are energized, balanced, and attuned mentally, physically, and spiritually.*

Aside from energizing and protecting the group, this procedure can be highly useful in motivating the group and increasing its commitment to specific purposes and goals. Step 4 of the procedure can be easily modified to focus the group's energies on highly specific objectives. Groups with a particular mission have found the procedure useful in mobilizing their resources as well as gaining support from outside the group. The procedure is effective for conventional groups as well as cutting-edge organizations. Its applications range from self-improvement goals, such as weight management and stopping smoking, to broad cultural issues, such as protecting the environment and promoting world peace.

With only minor modifications, the Group Empowerment Procedure can be used as an effective psychic healing strategy. For that application, the procedure can be readily altered to include relevant healing goals and appropriate group focusing in which healing energy is projected to the designated recipient(s), whether present or at a distance.

Organizational Psychic Vampirism

Group psychic vampirism can become so rampant and ingrained that an entire organization or institution can acquire serious vampire traits, a condition we call *organizational psychic vampirism*. This type of vampirism can be found in many industrial organizations and established institutions in which the structured, collective efforts of the organized group (especially the leadership) take on serious psychic vampire motives and characteristics.

In contrast to other forms of psychic vampirism, organizational psychic vampirism uses vampire tactics, either consciously or subconsciously, to achieve the goals of a formally organized group, often under the leadership of top-management personnel who have a long history of one-on-one psychic vampirism. While organizational psychic vampirism manifests in organized form some of the same characteristics of one-on-one vampirism, it affects larger numbers of people, with consequences of cultural, and even global, implications.

In one-on-one psychic vampirism, the typical vampire is usually content to muster the minimal amount of energy required for an attack in order to replenish and energize a deficient energy system. The energy gained by the attack is usually sufficient to replace the expended energy while enriching, at least temporarily, the vampire's energy system with a fresh supply of new energy. In contrast, organizational vampirism focuses its massive resources on explicit goals with destructive and sometimes deadly consequences. Its strategies often include large-scale manipulation, exploitation, and deception of target populations.

Organizational psychic vampirism can be a powerful force that influences the total organization and its internal structure as well as large numbers of persons outside the organization. Vampire organizations typically focus their efforts and resources to create potentially destructive "group vampire pressures" that influence the thoughts, perceptions, and behaviors of the internal organization as well as target populations. Of course, almost all organizations deliberately organize and focus their efforts and resources, but they meet the criteria for vampirism only when their strategies are irresponsible, deceptive, and detrimental in some way.

A familiar example of massive psychic vampirism today is organized crime. Often international in scope, organized crime drains community resources and destroys lives. Its modus operandi include illicit drug trafficking; smuggling; counterfeiting; extortion; robbery; fraud; bribery; kidnapping; arson; murder; prostitution; loan sharking; and other illegal acts of exploitation and terror. While its affluent leaders have in some instances become folk heroes, its prime motive is wealth through destructive exploitation with absolutely no regard for the human misery it breeds.

Rising arguably to the same level as organized crime is psychic vampirism found among many established corporations. Corporate vampirism, as it could be called, results from the deliberate decision of the organic corporation to engage in predatory corporate activities, typically for profit. Corporate vampirism can become so ingrained that it affects the structure, policies, and procedures of the total organization. Although cloaked in respectability, predator corporations have been known to vigorously market products known to be dangerous and, in some instances, potentially fatal to consumers. A common practice among vampire-entrenched corporations is to either ignore or deny altogether the health or safety risks associated with their products, often through promotional and advertising practices that include stonewalling and outright deception.

A prime example of corporate psychic vampirism is Big Tobacco. Its long history of predatory marketing practices in promoting the use of tobacco products while denying their known addictive and dangerous nature has unmistakable fingerprints of psychic vampirism. The vampire driven industry's determination to protect itself and promote its product at any cost, even at sacrificing the health and lives of consumers (including children) rather than developing a safer, nonaddictive product, is corporate vampirism in its most vicious and disgraceful form. The industry's use of cartoon characters and candy cigarettes that target children are only two examples that reflect the shameful callousness to which Big Tobacco can stoop. Sadly, its vampire tactics usually worked. Research, for instance, found that children who consumed candy cigarettes were twice as likely to take up smoking, even when their parents were nonsmokers. The enthusiastic cooperation of intercollegiate and professional sports—also driven by the profit motive in its promotion of tobacco products—is equally as sordid and outrageous. Likewise, many retail organizations, including nationwide pharmacies, are culpable for their willingness to promote the widespread use of a dangerous, addictive product. Ironically, many of the same pharmacies, including nationwide chains that sell health products and prescribed medicines at the rear blatantly sell health-hazardous tobacco products at the front. Hopefully, conscientious pharmacists everywhere will soon rise together as responsible professionals to protest and eliminate this outrageous practice. Without doubt, health care professionals of the future will look back in astonishment at this widespread vampire practice of promoting a known health-risk product for profit.

The predatory practices of vampire corporations can include vampire sins of omission as well as sins of commission, typically to increase profits. Examples are failure of manufacturers to disclose known health and safety risks associated with their products and, equally as disturbing, delaying their recall of products known to pose serious risks to the consumer. In litigation prior to the recall of dangerous consumer products, the terms of court settlements and the evidence upon which they were base are all too often unavailable to the consumer. Finally, when the product is reluctantly recalled, the company's public relations wheels begin their vampire spin to regain consumer confidence and reclaim their friendly, generous corporate image.

Aside from the deliberate production and marketing of products known to be harmful, corporate vampirism can assume a variety of other shapes and forms. A common example is dangerous work conditions that put company employees and, in some instances, the general public at risk. Unfortunately, conscientious whistle-blowers in the corporate vampire setting often find their careers and even their lives at risk.

A very recent example of flagrant psychic vampirism in the corporate setting is the collapse of Enron, the world's largest energy-trading company. Its vampire tactics included, among other things, outright deception by overstating company profits and providing other inaccurate information to insiders and outsiders alike. Even more outrageous, the failing company's top executives made millions by frantically selling off stock before the company's impending collapse while, at the same time, vampirizing beleaguered employees by restricting them from selling their 401(k) company stock until its value fell from a $90 high to only 26 cents. As it turns out, Enron's arrogant, deal-making vampire schemes led to the biggest—and possibly most scandalous—corporate bankruptcy in U.S. history.

Surprisingly, even academic institutions are not exempt from psychic vampirism. Institutions of higher learning are expected to champion knowledge and contribute to public enlightenment. Instead, academic institutions have too often nurtured academic vampirism—a subtle parasite that wastes the institution's resources and dilutes the quality of its programs. The first symptoms of academic vampirism are resistance to accountability and lack of commitment to academic excellence. Responsible educators everywhere agree that a strong commitment to excellence is a reasonable expectation for any academic institution. Unfortunately, the victim of academic vampirism is not the impersonal institution, but rather the student who is denied a quality education.

For any group, organization, or institution, organized involvement in rewarding activities and interactions is one of the best and most productive energizing strategies known. It follows that establishing positive goals and promoting involvement in achieving them are critical to any group, organization, or institution. They not only promote growth, they consistently repel the threat of vampirism from within and without.

Global Psychic Vampirism

Beyond groups, organizations, and institutions, psychic vampirism can occur on a massive, global scale. Human strivings in the global settings—including finding solutions to global problems and resolving international conflicts—are often influenced by the collective energies of nations and their leaders. By organizing the energies and resources of large numbers of persons, leaders throughout history have literally shaped global events. All too frequently, however, vampire leaders and power groups have drained critical resources from large populations, sometimes depriving them of their cultural traditions and even life itself as tragically seen in the Holocaust and, more recently, "ethnic cleansings"—even as the world looked on.

While the most vicious manifestation of global psychic vampirism is the organized destruction of other human beings, it can take many other forms. Common examples of contemporary global vampirism are the widespread abuses of human rights, reckless exploitation of our natural resources, environmental pollution, and worldwide poverty, to list but a few. Like insatiable vampires, these conditions and the leaders who promote them deplete the human potential for growth and global progress. Unfortunately, whenever psychic vampirism exists on a global scale, it is usually rampant in its other forms as well.

Civilization at any moment in time is the product of its present strivings as well as the cumulation of its past. Like each of us, civilization progressively generates a dynamic global record—an archive that chronicles its existence from its earliest beginnings to the present. Recorded in bold relief on a global scale are civilization's accomplishments and victories as well as its failures and defeats. While we exist only in the present, any unresolved legacy of our past demands our attention and resolution. Throughout history, our potential for compassion and commitment to the common good has all too often been offset by tyranny, savagery, and war. Past and present global atrocities and abuses of human rights weave an ominous vampire cape that continues to eclipse the globe.

War is perhaps the most vicious global vampire of all. Early in our nation's history, Thomas Paine recognized the vampire nature of war: "He who is the author of a war lets loose the whole contagion of hell and opens a vein that bleeds a nation to death." Within the sphere of human activity, war more than any other event thwarts global progress and deranges the course of human life. An emblem of misery, it disrupts balance by generating destructive energy on a massive scale that can shroud the earth for decades. To quote Ben Franklin, "There never was a good war or a bad peace." War is political murder that builds on old corruption and generates new corruption. It takes decades to build peace, but only seconds to destroy it. War, like peace, originates within us. More than ever before, we must bend every energy to prevent war and build peace.

On a massive scale, we continue to struggle under the weight of oppressive global baggage that slows our progress toward realization of our personal and global potentials. The dark side of human nature and the potential for depravity are vampire weights that demand our awareness and action.

Faithfully counterbalancing the dark record of our past is the nurturing side of humanity. Despite our failures, the globe eventually moves forward. Largely because of the human struggle to grow and survive, the world today is an improvement over the past. But progress is never easy. Against the backdrop of our past, present global challenges constantly demand our very best.

The globe is more than a stage upon which we are players; it is an active teacher whose methods at once challenge and liberate. At a personal level, a major task now facing each of us is to promote global progress while countering global regression. By energizing the globe, we can defeat global vampirism in whatever its form. Together, we can make the world a richer, safer place for ourselves and future generations. Right now, we have all the resources we need to accomplish that important task.

Global Empowerment Procedure

The Global Empowerment Procedure is used as a group activity to generate a bright, new energy force sufficient to energize the earth and repel the dark forces that constrict it and erode its resources. The procedure amasses large amounts of energy and focuses it on the earth as the essential environment for human growth and fulfillment. By enveloping the earth with new energy and power, it engenders a global actualization process that benefits everyone. At the same time, it protects the earth from disempowering forces—including global vampirism—that impede personal growth and global progress.

The procedure requires the physical presence of a globe model of the earth positioned so as to be visible to the total group. The procedure is built on the premise that interacting with the globe model can become a gateway to interacting with the planet. Having first focused on energizing the globe as a miniature representation of the earth, the group shifts its focus on energizing the earth itself. The procedure concludes with a powerful cosmic event in which the group as well as the earth is infused with powerful cosmic energy. The procedure is practiced step-by-step by the full group.

Step 1. Viewing the Globe. Together with the group, view the globe model and, while focusing your attention on it, clear your mind of active thought. Sense your connection to the globe model as a replica of the earth. Affirm that by first interacting with the globe model, you can interact with the earth.

Step 2. Energizing the Globe Model. Gently rub your hands together as you sense warm energy building between them. Turn your palms outward so that they face the globe model, and allow the energy emanating from your palms to envelop it. As the group's energy infuses the globe model, a visible glow can often be seen around it, a manifestation in miniature of the group's power to energize the earth.

Step 3. Visualizing the Earth. Together with the group, close your eyes and visualize the earth with its oceans, rivers, mountains, plains, and so forth. Sense your connection to the earth as a cosmic creation and a habitat for growth.

Step 4. Energizing the Earth. As in Step 2, gently rub your hands together again and sense warm energy building between them. Turn your palms outward, moving them from side to side, and allow the energy in your palms to go forth, joining the energy of the group, to envelop the earth. As the glow of energy envelops the earth, focus on particular regions or populations and saturate them with energy.

Step 5. Cosmic Self-infusion. Turn the palms of your hands upward and visualize the distant core of the universe as a glowing orb of powerful energy. Sense your connection to that orb as the energizing source of your existence until your total being is filled and overflowing with cosmic energy.

Step 6. Global Cosmic Infusion. Let the inner infusion of cosmic energy expand to join the energies of the group, and then reach outward to further infuse the earth with powerful cosmic energy.

Step 7. Group Affirmation. Bring your hands together in a praying-hands position as you affirm in unison with the group: *I, along with the full earth, am energized, balanced, and attuned. I am at one with the cosmos.*

Step 8. Personal Affirmation. Affirm that by simply bringing your hands together as you envision the energizing core of the cosmos, you can instantly activate the full empowering potential of this exercise.

Aside from its stated objective of energizing and protecting the earth, this procedure is particularly effective in promoting group cohesiveness and productivity. Organizations that practice the procedure regularly become more globally oriented and focused. Their vision of possibilities, not only for the group but for the earth, expands. They become more effective in meeting the group's goals while actively promoting progress on a global scale.

Becoming an empowered group in an empowered world is any group's best defense against psychic vampirism or any other opposing force. Groups everywhere, regardless of their makeup, will find the two procedures presented in this chapter both group-empowering and personally rewarding.

Summary

This chapter examined group psychic vampirism, which differs from other forms of vampirism in that it involves either multiple vampires or multiple victims and in some instances, it involves both.

Our group interactions often produce a synergistic effect in which the energy generated exceeds the sum of its contributing parts, a phenomenon which has been demonstrated in controlled PK laboratory experiments.

Group vampirism is often observed in competitive sports where it is usually seen as justifiable vampirism, since opposing teams are expected to dominate and de-energize each other. Group vampirism not of a justifiable nature often occurs in the work setting in which the psychic vampire drains energy from coworkers. It is also observed at times in the family setting where vampire-like strategies can include manipulation, defiance, hostility, and excessive control.

Group psychic vampirism can involve such strategies as surfing and infiltration, both of which are deliberately structured to draw energy from a group and interrupt its functions. The Group Empowerment Procedure is effective in protecting the group from both surfing and infiltration, while motivating the group and infusing it with fresh new energy.

Organizational vampirism is collective vampirism that is observed in certain major corporations that take on vampire-like traits and practices. Familiar examples are corporations that irresponsibly pollute the environment, as well as corporations whose products pose health or safety risks to consumers.

Global vampirism is the most massive form of psychic vampirism known. Occurring on a global scale, it drains critical resources from large populations. Examples are abuses of human rights, exploitation of children, oppression of selected groups, and worldwide poverty. In its worst form, it can involve the organized destruction of other human being on a massive scale. The Global Empowerment Procedure is designed to energize and protect the earth from global vampirism.

SIX

Parasitic Vampirism

IMAGINE A TENACIOUS inner force that can become so intense that it overpowers the person like a bloodthirsty vampire. Strange as it might at first seem, such an oppressive force exists—it is called *parasitic vampirism*. It subtly attaches itself like a parasite to its victims, and once firmly in place it relentlessly dominates and drives them with grinding intensity. It is vampirism in one of its most common yet potentially damaging forms.

Parasitic vampirism is psychic vampirism turned inward against oneself rather than outward against others. It is so powerful and so potentially harmful that, if left unchallenged, it can become a constricting inner force with seemingly a life of its own. It can arrest growth, damage the internal energy system, and drain its victim of the vital resources required for daily functioning. Once their inner resources are exhausted, victims of parasitic vampirism have been known to turn to one-on-one psychic vampirism in a desperate effort to meet their energy needs. That insatiable combination is doubly destructive—it devours one's own energies as well as the energies of others.

Although the concept of parasitic vampirism was introduced several decades ago as a way to explain compulsive mechanisms that drive the anxiety patient, it was not widely used, possibly because of its narrow focus and limited relevance. As a result of studies conducted in our laboratories at Athens State University, the concept of parasitic vampirism has been significantly expanded, and its underlying dynamics have been more clearly defined. Even more importantly, new prevention and treatment strategies for parasitic vampirism have been developed and are now available to everyone, as we will later see.

In its current usage, parasitic vampirism includes any internal process or condition that wastes our energy resources, erodes our internal energy system, and disrupts our personal development. In its myriad of forms, several of which we will later discuss, parasitic vampirism creates a vicious inner cycle with a insatiable appetite—the more it consumes, the more it demands. It nibbles away at our inner resources and, in the long haul, it exacts a devastating toll on the quality of our lives.

It is important to emphasize that the vampire in parasitic vampirism is not the person, but rather the process. It not only consumes its victim's energy, it maintains an inner state of weakness and vulnerability. That two-fold function suggests a two-fold solution—first, correcting the underlying conditions that contribute to parasitic vampirism; and second, directly fortifying the internal energy system. The first solution focuses on cause; whereas the second focuses on effect. We will later present step-by-step procedures that are designed to achieve these important goals.

Like other forms of psychic vampirism, we all possess at least some of the characteristics associated with parasitic vampirism. Examples are unresolved conflicts, unwanted habits, self-defeating emotions such as jealousy and hostility, persistent fears, and a myriad of other anxieties, each of which increases our vulnerability to parasitic vampirism. We could add to these a host of stressful life events that test our endurance, deplete our coping resources, and interfere in our well-being. While these adverse conditions are enfeebling when we succumb to them, they are empowering when we encounter and overcome them. They signal parasitic vampirism only when we are dominated or controlled by them.

Unfortunately, anyone can become the victim of parasitic vampirism. It can develop slowly over a period of years, or it can surface in full-blown, all-consuming intensity. A severely traumatic life event, for instance, can be so devastating that our coping mechanisms are instantly shattered. We can become at once vulnerable and defenseless. On the other hand, our adjustment mechanisms can gradually deteriorate over time, often because of long-term stress. Even at moderate levels, stress can slowly consume our energy resources while asserting a wear-and-tear effect on the energy system itself. It can accelerate aging and affect our concentration, memory, and performance. It can strain the body's critical organs and overload their functions. Today, it is estimated that at least 80 percent of all physical illnesses are related to stress. Stress has been implicated in disorders such as cancer, diabetes, heart disease, and stroke, to list but a few. Stress can accelerate aging and diminish the quality of life. Difficult transitions, such as divorce, loss of job, midlife crises, and even retirement can generate stress and sand down our capacity to cope with it, thus providing fertile conditions for parasitic vampirism to flourish. When harbored within the self and denied release, stress can reach levels that are self-devouring. Because stress is so widespread and destructive, effective stress management is a critical component of any plan to combat parasitic vampirism. We will later present step-by-step stress management procedures designed specifically to counteract parasitic vampirism.

As a driving inner force, full-blown parasitic vampirism persistently consumes our energies, often leaving behind not only fatigue but also a vacuum of crippling despondency, meaninglessness, and despair. Perhaps not surprisingly, victims of extreme parasitic vampirism often describe themselves as "a shell of a person." Slowly and relentlessly, psychic vampirism dashes hope and devours peace of mind. When unchallenged, it spawns unhappiness, fear, and despair.

In its severest form, it can maliciously wound the spirit and lead to zombie-like estrangement from one's self and the world. That mind-numbing sense of detachment from one's mind and body, often called *depersonalization,* is one of the most devastating effects of parasitic vampirism. Sadly, by surrendering to parasitic vampirism rather than confronting it, we relinquish our struggle for meaning and our claim to personal fulfillment.

In contrast to an empowered energy system that fuels our growth and promotes a sense of personal worth, parasitic vampirism enfeebles the energy system and constantly wastes our energies and growth resources. In the worst scenario, it inflicts serious damage to the energy system itself. As a result, we become mentally, physically, and spiritually victimized by vampirism in a virulent form that knows no bounds.

Typically, the first casualty of parasitic vampirism is our sense of adequacy, security, and well-being. Deficient of these essentials, we tend to turn to unworkable coping strategies that further deplete our energy reserves and draw us into a suction-like conundrum that exacts an even greater toll on our coping resources. A vicious dilemma, which we call the *parasitic vampire cycle,* unfolds: Failed attempts to cope with vampire threats against our well-being lead to even greater anxiety, insecurity, and vulnerability, all of which further diminish our ability to cope. The result is an unrelenting struggle within the self, one of the major characteristics of parasitic vampirism.

Parasitic vampirism reaches its peak when either our energy resources are finally exhausted or the struggle becomes unbearable. The results can range from insulated withdrawal to excruciating distress that seems to be without end. Almost always underlying these surface manifestations are feelings of inadequacy and insecurity that help fuel parasitic vampirism.

Parasitic Vampire Mechanisms

Like a masked tormentor quite capable of inflicting serious harm upon its victim, parasitic vampirism cloaks itself in a variety of energy-consuming mechanisms. Among the most common are phobias, obsessions, compulsions, and the parasitic anxiety state—each of which exhausts valuable resources that could otherwise be mobilized to promote our growth and enrich the quality of our lives.

Parasitic Phobias

One of the most flagrant consumers of our energy resources is the *parasitic phobia*—an irrational, persistent fear of objects or situations. Even when we are not exposed to the phobic condition, the phobia persists—often because of fear that future exposure is somehow imminent. Perhaps it is not merely coincidental that persons with parasitic phobias, when asked to draw pictures depicting their fears, often draw dark, vampire-like creatures hovering over them as if ominously waiting to devour them.

Parasitic phobias can be so intense that they can seriously impair our ability to achieve important life goals. This was illustrated by a college student whose fear of heights was so intense that his graduation was delayed because of his inability to attend classes other than those held at ground-floor levels. When asked to draw a picture depicting his phobia, he drew a lifeless human figure in the clutches of a dark bat. Each essential element in his drawing held relevance to his fear. The bat symbolized the vampire nature of his fear; an ominous cloud hovering over the bat symbolized his persistent feelings of hopelessness; sharply pointed structures on the ground below symbolized inescapable danger; and the lifeless figure in the bat's clutches represented himself as the helpless victim of fear.

Parasitic phobias are characterized not only by avoidance of whatever is feared, but severe discomfort during exposure, a condition we call the *parasitic phobic attack*. The attack is usually accompanied by overwhelming fear along with such reactions as sweating, trembling, nausea, and chest pains. In extreme cases, encountering the feared situation can be so distressful that death seems near at hand. As with one-on-one vampirism, physical exhaustion following the vampire phobic attack is common.

Parasitic phobias are important to our study of psychic vampirism for several reasons. First, they are very common, and they require enormous amounts of energy to sustain them. Equally as important, parasitic phobias can cause distress so severe that they strain the energy system and impair its capacity to function. Parasitic phobias are almost always long-term. Quite often they are reactions to either childhood trauma or painful past-life experiences. Here are some examples of common phobias with parasitic vampire elements.

Parasitic Social Phobia—The marked fear of social situations, which can include public performances ("stage fright") and threatening social interactions. Often emerging in the mid-teens, social phobias can become like clinging, lifelong vampires that limit our activities, consume our energies, and erode our coping capacity. Fear of being embarrassed or judged to be anxious is central to most social phobias.

Parasitic Death Phobia—A morbid fear of dying. In parasitic vampirism, this fear is often accompanied by feelings of worthlessness and guilt. Our studies found that sudden death by accident or assassination in a recent past-life is often associated with this fear.

Parasitic Hypochrondriacal Phobia—Fear of having a serious organic disease despite medical reassurance. In parasitic vampirism, this fear is often linked to an inadequate self-image and exaggerated concern regarding one's physical appearance.

Parasitic Monophobia—Fear of being alone. In parasitic vampirism, this fear is associated with feelings of vulnerability, fear of abandonment, and the need for support or reassurance.

Parasitic Ochlophobia—Fear of crowds. In parasitic vampirism, this fear is linked to distrust and feelings of alienation. Our past-life regression studies found that public execution in a past life was often related to this phobia.

Parasitic Claustrophobia—Fear of closed spaces. In parasitic vampirism, this widespread fear is sometimes associated with having been buried alive in a past life. Supportive of this possibility is the fact that premature burials were common in the United States well into the twentieth century, with estimates of at least one live burial a week.

Parasitic Hematophobia—Fear of blood. In hematophobia, the sight of blood, particularly if flowing or spilled, evokes fear of injury, pain, or death. In parasitic vampirism, this phobia can be so intense that it can result in either panic or fainting at the sight of blood.

The above are only a few of many phobias with parasitic vampire elements. Theoretically, any fear that wastes our energy resources, interferes in our well-being, and impairs our ability to cope could be considered parasitic vampirism. Whatever the phobia and the vampire process associated with it, the empowerment strategies presented later in this chapter have been effective in counteracting parasitic fear and its enfeebling effects on the energy system.

Parasitic Obsessions and Compulsions

Aside from phobias, parasitic vampirism can include a wide range of obsessions and compulsions that waste our energy resources and interfere in our daily lives. *Parasitic obsessions* are repetitively intruding thoughts, impulses, emotions, or images that insistently force their way into our conscious awareness, even though they are unwanted. *Parasitic compulsions,* on the other hand, are acts of behavior that repeatedly intrude into our lives. When extreme and long-lived, both of these mechanisms can become a never-ending parasitic harassment. They are like vampire tentacles that tap our energy resources and force us into a variety of maneuvers in a vain effort to avoid or remove them.

Parasitic obsessions usually function as defenses against unacceptable motives or drives buried deeply in the subconscious. For instance, a "meaningless" thought that runs over and over in our mind can occupy conscious space and awareness, thereby protecting us from the intrusion of unacceptable subconscious urges. Like a stuck phonograph record, the senseless thought stays in the same groove, commanding our attention and consuming our energies, while at the same time holding the rejected urge at bay. Unfortunately, the unwanted thought itself can become a source of increased anxiety, thus energizing the rejected urge and kick-starting the all-too-common parasitic vampire cycle.

Like phobias, many parasitic obsessions seem to result from painful experiences, which can be of either present- or past-life origin. They are often image-related obsession consisting of very vivid, highly detailed images of the traumatic experience. An example is the French scientist and philosopher Pascal, who always thought that he saw an abyss in his left hand after a near-death experience in which his coach was almost thrown into the Seine.

Parasitic obsessions of past-life origin are almost always image related, as illustrated by a forty-two-year-old chemist whose obsession consisted of recurring images of flowing lava. During a past-life regression, he re-experienced a tragedy in which his village was destroyed by a volcanic eruption. He was the only member of his family to have survived the catastrophe. In another instance, an attorney experienced an obsessive image of a very high cliff, particularly upon meeting someone toward whom she felt physically attracted. Always accompanying the image was a mysterious pressure in her left hand. Through past-life regression, she discovered that in a past life she had leaped from a cliff to her death with her young lover as he firmly held her left hand.

Along a totally different line, parasitic obsessions often involve an extreme preoccupation with the physical body, including a particular physical characteristic, organ, or function. In parasitic vampirism, these so-called somatic obsessions are preoccupations that are usually associated with an inadequate self-concept and poor physical body image. The somatic obsession can become a vampire circuit through which we interact with others, thereby limiting our perceptions and constricting our relationships. For instance, a person who thinks constantly of his large nose operates within a distracting "nose circuit." In relating to others, he sees only their noses and compares them with his own. Common among somatic obsessions are hair (or its absence), muscles, ears, complexion, height, and weight. Empowerment procedures related to somatic obsessions are designed to address faulty self-perceptions and inferiority feelings that often underlie and energize the somatic obsession.

One of the most interesting and complex obsessions related to parasitic vampirism is the masked obsession. In this case, the parasitic obsession appears in the disguised form of other symptoms. Common examples are complaints of pain with no organic cause. The pain can provide a convenient mask for a pleasurable but unacceptable memory, typically of a sexual nature. Masked by pain, the memory remains hidden, yet it continues to consume energy by sustaining the pain.

As with many other parasitic obsessions, the masked obsession often consists of repressed experiences that generate energy-consuming guilt. An extreme yet common example is guilt and hopelessness resulting from the obsession of having committed "the unpardonable sin." Even when the obsession remains hidden, the guilt and hopelessness masking it can be so intense that it drives the person to despair and in some instances, even suicide. Unfortunately, certain organized religions have too often fostered this form of destructive vampirism. (A recent survey of church ministers in the so-called Bible Belt found that 63 percent of them believed it was possible to commit the unpardonable sin, and over half of them believed it was a common occurrence.) Parasitic vampirism, like other forms of vampirism, can indeed involve matters of life and death significance.

Although it may at first seem far-fetched, there is some evidence to suggest that obsessions are sometimes carried over from this life into the afterlife or discarnate realm. If, as already suggested, certain obsessions survive from life to life, it would seem plausible that they could remain active between lives as well. That possibility would explain apparitions that recur for many years, particularly at sites of untimely or tragic death. The recurring apparition could represent the discarnate's obsessive need to right a wrongful act or else make some sense of a past-life tragedy. There are, of course, many other possible explanations for recurring apparitions. Nevertheless, certain discarnate manifestations do seem to suggest that our passing over to the other side does not always instantly disarm the mechanisms related to parasitic vampirism. It follows that developing our capacity to effectively counteract parasitic vampirism is important, both for now and the future. Fortunately, the procedures that liberate and protect us from parasitic vampirism are not time sensitive—they have no expiration date. Once mastered, they become permanent resources that are an integral part of our being.

Unlike obsessions, parasitic compulsions as previously noted are intruding acts of behavior that feed on our energy resources. Parasitic compulsions can be described as obsessions in action. Among the common examples are excessive counting, hand washing, rechecking, and silently repeating certain words or phrases over and over again. Even though we do not wish to perform the act, the need forces itself upon us anyway. Hence once again, a vicious, seemingly inescapable parasitic vampire cycle emerges. Although performing the compulsion creates anxiety, failure to perform it leads to even greater anxiety.

When combined, parasitic obsessions and compulsions interact to form a doubly destructive condition that overloads our energy system and critically depletes our energy resources. While parasitic obsessions generate marked anxieties, parasitic compulsions attempt, albeit unsuccessfully, to reduce or neutralize them. For instance, the obsession of being contaminated by germs is often accompanied by the compulsion to wash one's hands every few minutes. Unfortunately, the relief provided by the compulsion is only temporary if at all. The result is an even more vicious vampire cycle in which mounting anxiety evokes the obsession and related compulsion with even greater intensity and frequency.

Like other forms of parasitic vampirism, obsessive-compulsive reactions can be so severe that they totally exhaust our inner resource and finally erode our ability to generate new energy required for daily functioning. Because they are often excessive and unusual, they can markedly interfere with our careers and relationships. Simple compulsive counting, for instance, can interrupt concentration and the task at hand; excessive cleanliness can consume tremendous time and energy essential for other tasks; and rigidly structuring each daily activity not only consumes time and energy, it eliminates spontaneity and creativity.

But while obsessive-compulsive reactions are intrusive and exhaustive, they are not usually within easy range of our conscious control. They can involve deep-seated subconscious motives and complicated mechanisms that are difficult to untangle. Nevertheless, as we will later see, the subconscious is a willing collaborator in our efforts to break the inner cycle of parasitic vampirism, regardless of its source.

It is important again to emphasize that not all phobias, obsessions, compulsions, and other anxiety conditions signal full-blown parasitic vampirism. As already noted, we all possess to some extent certain characteristics that could be associated with parasitic vampirism. But only when the condition is sufficiently severe as to seriously deplete our adjustment resources, consume our coping energies, and impair important areas of our lives does it suggest full-blown parasitic vampirism. Fortunately, the intervention strategies that are now available to break the harsh grip of parasitic vampirism are equally as useful in preventing it in the first place.

Parasitic Anxiety State

Aside from phobias, obsessions, and compulsions, parasitic vampirism can include a general state of unrelenting anxiety, which is accompanied by a variety of negative emotions, unresolved conflicts, faulty self-perceptions, and physical symptoms that significantly impair our ability to function. More specifically, the symptoms can include restlessness, difficulty concentrating, sleep disturbances, worry, and feelings of insecurity and inferiority. Common among the physical symptoms are weakness and fatigue, tension headaches, muscle tension, numbness or tingling sensations, and abdominal distress. The parasitic anxiety state can be punctuated by intense anxiety attacks which are characterized by intense fear, panic, and discomfort along with many of the same symptoms observed among victims of the one-on-one vampire attack. The attack and resultant exhaustion can be so severe that a recovery period is required.

Parasitic Vampirism in the Laboratory

Conducted over the past quarter century, our pioneering studies of parasitic vampirism consisted of two stages. Stage 1 focused on the origin, progression, and dynamics of the phenomenon; whereas Stage 2 focused on developing practical prevention and intervention strategies. This sequence of stages was based on the general premise that the better our understanding of any phenomenon, including parasitic vampirism, the more effective our efforts in developing relevant empowerment procedures.

The techniques used in Stage 1 to investigate the basic nature of parasitic vampirism consisted of personal interviews, case studies, and hypnosis. Participants for this stage were all volunteers drawn from the college student population. Interviews using a structured interview guide were conducted with each participant in an effort to identify the existence of parasitic vampire symptoms. For subjects identified with relevant symptoms, the case study was used to investigate contributing background and situational factors. Finally, hypnosis was used to uncover contributing subconscious elements, including past-life experiences.

Among the earliest findings of our studies was the critical importance of self-image. It became almost instantly apparent that a poor self-concept—including feelings of inferiority, alienation, and helplessness—almost always accompanies parasitic vampirism. Other characteristics found to be commonly associated with parasitic vampirism were a pessimistic outlook, distrust and resentment of others, and deep-seated conflicts. Background factors often included a history of failed relationships and unstable family conditions.

Our use of hypnosis to explore parasitic vampirism was based on the view that underlying our conscious behavior is a vast region of subconscious motives and drives. Through hypnosis, we can explore that region and uncover explanations for behaviors—including parasitic vampirism—that would otherwise remain puzzling to us. Equally as important, hypnosis holds promise as an intervention strategy to activate our subconscious powers while resolving the conflicts that fuel parasitic vampirism. (In a later chapter, we will present step-by-step procedures that use self-hypnosis to counteract psychic vampirism in its various forms.)

Hypnosis, along with case-study results, identified several interesting defense strategies commonly found in parasitic vampirism. Designed to meet situation demands while conserving energy, the strategies were basically ineffective—they sometimes worked for awhile, but they did not resolve the underlying issues. Instead, they tended to either break down or become exaggerated, conditions that actually increased vulnerability to psychic vampirism. As it turns out, the parasitic mechanisms designed to conserve energy actually consumed more energy, thus perpetuating the vicious parasitic vampire cycle. Here are examples of common parasitic defense strategies that are essentially self-defeating.

> **Vampire Avoidance.** This strategy selectively avoids unpleasant tasks and situations that demand energy. Characteristic particularly of phobias, the strategy can include complaints of fatigue to avoid dealing with problems, either exaggerating problems or denying their existence altogether, and avoiding responsibility by excessively depending on others. In couples' relations, this parasitic pattern can lead to a frustrating form of one-on-one psychic vampirism with one's partner, thus weakening the relationship and, in some instances, literally destroying it.

> **Vampire Forgetting.** Sometimes called "motivated forgetting," this strategy, like vampire avoidance, is used to escape demanding situations that tax one's energy supply. A common example is conveniently forgetting unpleasant appointments and events in an effort to conserve energy. A common strategy associated with vampire forgetting is scheduling

unpleasant events as far into the future as possible in order to subconsciously promote forgetting.

Vampire Aggression. This is a form of low-energy aggression often found in the occupational setting. Typically passive in nature, vampire aggression in the workplace includes excessive absences, procrastination, complaints of unfair treatment, failing to meet deadlines, being overly critical of coworkers and superiors, and manipulating others into perform one's assigned tasks ("you-can-do-it-better-than-I" syndrome). Vampire aggression in social situations outside the workplace is also typically passive, with such patterns as aloofness, detachment, and insensibility being common. Vampire aggression can also include feigning illness to obtain special treatment or attention.

Vampire Self-promotion. These are low-energy strategies such as excuses, manipulation, and deception designed to promote oneself. Examples are taking credit for the accomplishments of others, exaggerating one's credentials and achievements, and finding plausible excuses for one's failures or shortcomings.

Underlying each of these mechanisms are a poor self-image, lack of self-insight, and, of course, inefficiency in meeting one's energy needs.

Our use of hypnosis in Stage 1 found that parasitic vampirism almost always has its roots in experiences buried deep in the subconscious. Hypnotic age-regression in which the subject was taken back in time to re-experience childhood events confirmed many of our case-study findings concerning the importance of the early developmental years. Especially critical were early traumatic experiences that, once lost to conscious awareness, later manifest themselves through a variety of anxiety symptoms. It would follow that any solution to parasitic vampirism must include exploration of the subconscious forces that help fuel the condition. Only through increased awareness and insight can many of the shackles of parasitic vampirism be finally broken.

A major purpose of hypnosis in Phase 1 was to determine the relevance of past-life experiences to parasitic vampirism. Hypnotic past-life regression often uncovered critical past-life events directly related to parasitic vampirism. For instance, the accumulation of painful past-life experiences, such as being outcast and homeless, often resurfaced in a future lifetime as parasitic vampirism in the form of deep insecurity and fear of abandonment. Similarly, our studies found that unresolved past-life experiences were often the source of parasitic phobias. Especially critical were unresolved conflicts and trauma associated with sudden death or other tragedy. Here are some specific instances of phobias related to past-life experiences as uncovered in our studies.

- Stage fright and fear of crowds were reactions to death by public execution in a past life.
- Claustrophobia and fear of suffocating resulted from having been buried alive in a past life. As noted earlier, reports of premature burials were common in the United States even into the twentieth century.
- Fears of rats, spiders, and crawling insects were associated with having spent time in a dungeon in a past life.
- Fear of sunset accompanied by depression at sunset was a reaction to execution by hanging at sunset in a past life.
- Fear of blood was a reaction to medical treatment involving bloodletting and resultant death in a past life.
- Fear of bright sunlight, along with the compulsion of wearing dark shades even when indoors, was related to past-life torture in which the eyelids were cut away and the subject was left to die in the desert with arms bound behind his back.
- Fear of heights and bridges was associated with having fallen to one's death from a bridge in a past life.

Along a somewhat different line, certain past-life events were found to give rise in a future lifetime to parasitic obsessions and compulsions. Here are some specific examples uncovered in our studies.

- For a nineteen-year-old chemistry major, death resulting from the plague generated a future-life obsession of being contaminated by germs and the compulsion for excessive cleanliness, including repetitive hand-washing.

- For an art major, age twenty-two, shipwreck and death at sea in a past life resulted in obsessive sensory images (along with recurrent dreams) of clinging onto a piece of driftwood and floating aimlessly at sea. The sensory obsession had its intellectual counterpart of questioning the purpose of life and brooding about death.

- For a business major, age twenty-four, compulsive overeating was associated with a past life of extreme poverty and stealing food to survive. His compulsive behavior was accompanied by extreme competitiveness and overachievement, an apparent reaction to past-life poverty.

- For a prelaw major, age twenty-three, obsessive doubts and difficulty making decisions were reactions to past-life experiences as a military leader whose reckless strategies led to the deaths of the troops under his command.

Incredible as it may seem, our studies found that awareness of the past-life source of parasitic vampirism was often sufficient in and of itself to instantly extinguish the condition. This finding suggests that the past-life energizers of parasitic vampirism are effective only in their subconscious, repressed forms. Past-life enlightenment thus becomes a powerful force in ventilating and counteracting the parasitic vampire residue of painful past-life experiences. This finding held profound relevance to the next stage of our studies that focused on prevention and treatment.

Aside from extreme past-life events which seemed to activate parasitic vampirism in a future lifetime, certain past-life personality characteristics were found to provide sufficient reside for the future development of parasitic vampirism. If we are indeed the totality of our experiences, then not only our past-life experiences but also our acquired past-life personal traits—including strengths and weaknesses—could conceivably re-emerge in a future lifetime as past-life residue. Similarly, unfinished past-life tasks and unrealized growth potentials often persist as personal challenges in both the afterlife realm as well as in future lifetimes. Not surprisingly then, past-life personal baggage, including self-defeating attitudes and behavioral patterns, could carry over from life to life until we maximize our capacities to overcome or resolve them.

Our past-life regression studies of persons with severe parasitic vampire characteristics typically found oppressive baggage of past-life origin. In their past lives they tended to be insecure, fearful, and withdrawn. Often victims of oppression and persecution, they were distrustful and guarded in their past-life interactions with others. They were not, however, cruel, reckless despots who oppressed or exploited others, as was often the case with the full-blown person-to-person psychic vampire.

Based on the findings of Stage 1 of our studies, we developed the PV Self-rating Scale, a 25-item true/false test designed to measure parasitic vampire tendencies. As already noted, parasitic vampire symptoms, including anxiety, fear, poor self-perceptions, and insecurity, exist to some degree in everyone. But only when they reach levels that interfere in our daily activities, or when they are sufficiently intense as to appreciably reduce the quality of our lives, can they be considered relevant indicators of psychic vampirism. Here is the scale (see following page), which can be easily self-administered.

Using the scoring key, the higher the score on this test the higher the tendency toward parasitic vampirism. A score range of 20–25 suggests a severe tendency toward parasitic vampirism. A score range of 15–19 suggests a marked tendency toward parasitic vampirism. A score range of 10–14 suggests a moderate tendency toward parasitic vampirism. A score below 10 suggests no significant tendency toward parasitic vampirism.

PV Self-Rating Scale

Directions: Carefully read each of the following statements. If the statement is true or mostly true as applied to you, circle T. If the statement is false as applied to you, circle F.

T F 1. I am frequently irritable.

T F 2. I often feel that I am being influenced by forces beyond my control.

T F 3. I am bothered by the mistakes of my past.

T F 4. I am a person of value and worth.

T F 5. I am under a lot of pressure these days.

T F 6. I believe in my ability to shape my own future.

T F 7. I am a self-confident person.

T F 8. My inner struggles are so great that they are often overwhelming.

T F 9. Certain unwanted thoughts repeatedly enter my mind.

T F 10. I usually enjoy being around people.

T F 11. I have certain fears that are so intense that they seem beyond my control.

T F 12. I have great difficulty making important decisions.

T F 13. My life is full of meaning.

T F 14. I usually give in to people too easily.

T F 15. I have difficulty concentrating.

T F 16. I often have thoughts of ending my life.

T F 17. I am the unfortunate victim of circumstances.

T F 18. I am happy with my life.

T F 19. My life often seems hopeless.

T F 20. When I have a problem, I usually try not to think about it.

T F 21. I often feel my life is about to fall apart.

T F 22. I stay tired much of the time.

T F 23. I am disappointed at what I have been able to accomplish in life.

T F 24. I am optimistic about my future.

T F 25. I am easily discouraged.

Scoring Key: Allow one point for each of the following responses: Item 1 (T), 2 (T), 3(T), 4(F), 5(T), 6(F), 7(F), 8(T), 9(T), 10(F), 11(T), 12(T), 13(F), 14(T), 15(T), 16(T), 17(T), 18(F), 19(T), 20(T), 21(T), 22(T), 23(T), 24(F), 25(T).

The PV Self-rating Scale is structured to measure only tendencies toward parasitic vampirism, not for diagnostic classification or labeling. While a score range of 20 through 25 suggests a severe tendency toward parasitic vampirism, it does not indicate conclusively the existence of full-blown parasitic vampirism. In using this scale, whether for oneself or others, it is always important to keep in mind that we all possess certain tendencies that could be considered symptomatic of parasitic vampirism. As a footnote, you may have noted that the scale itself makes no reference to parasitic vampirism. This "blind" strategy is used in an effort to make the instrument as nonthreatening as possible, thus increasing its value as a self-rating scale.

In Stage 2 of our laboratory research, three major procedures were developed to counter parasitic vampirism. Each procedure includes certain mental, physical, and spiritual elements considered relevant to parasitic vampirism. The first procedure, the Stress Reduction Response, is a proactive procedure designed to eliminate negative stress, which is often at the core of parasitic vampirism, and replace it with positive self-perceptions designed to repel the invasion of psychic vampirism in any form. The second procedure, Corridor of Power, is a highly positive strategy designed to counteract parasitic vampire tendencies and activate the self's inner growth and protection potentials. The third procedure, Energy Replacement Strategy, is designed to target and replace specific parasitic agents—including phobias, obsessions, and compulsions—with an empowered state of well-being.

The Stress Reduction Response

The Stress Reduction Response, which requires a quiet, comfortable place, should be practiced at least once daily over at least a two-week period and then periodically as needed to reduce stress and fortify the self's vampire defense mechanisms. Everyone, including persons with no obvious tendency toward parasitic vampirism, can benefit from this strategy.

Step 1. **Mental Quietness.** With your eyes closed, breathe slowly and deeply as you clear your mind of active thought. Turn your thoughts inward, and find a quiet, still place somewhere within yourself. Take plenty of time to search your inner-most self until you find that special place. You will know the right place when you find it.

Step 2. **Settling In.** Once you find that inner place of quietness, settle into it, and let yourself become a part of it. Envision your presence in that space as a light form with the capacity to illuminate your total being. Let the brightness of your presence spread slowly throughout your being until you are fully infused with peace and tranquillity.

Step 3. **Physical Relaxation.** From your place of inner quiet-ness, mentally scan your physical body from your head downward. Pause briefly at any tense area and relax it by tak-ing in a deep breath and then slowly exhaling. Envision the area becoming illuminated with bright energy.

Step 4. **Cosmic Balance and Attunement.** Sense the cosmic part of your being reaching outward and connecting you to the higher cosmos. Visualize radiant beams emanating from your innermost being and reaching into infinity. Sense yourself becoming balanced with all that exists, from the innermost center of your being to the outermost reaches of the cosmos.

Step 5. **Empowerment Affirmations.** As you remain in your quiet, inner place, affirm: *I am balanced and attuned to the cos-mos. Peace is flowing gently throughout my total being. I am safe, protected, and secure.*

Step 6. **Fingertip Engagement.** Before opening your eyes, bring your hands together—fingertips against fingertips—as a sym-bolic gesture of inner peace and power.

Following sufficient practice of the full procedure, you can use the simple fingertip engagement gesture (Step 6) at will to energize, balance, and attune your total being.

Corridor of Power

The second procedure developed through our studies, Corridor of Power, focuses on extinguishing all existing parasitic vampire tendencies, including those with a long developmental history, by unleashing new growth potentials. Fortunately, we have an inner storehouse of abundant growth resources just waiting to be unleashed. Although instant eradication of deep-seated parasitic impulses has been known to occur from a single practice trial, this procedure usually requires considerable practice to maximize its effectiveness. Aside from those rare moments of enlightenment that initiate a totally new cycle of growth, most growth requires time, motivation, and, sometimes, hard work.

This procedure recognizes self-determination as the key that opens the door to new growth and power. We can deliberately choose new, more positive attitudes, perceptions, and behaviors. We can set new life goals and deliberately determine our life's destiny. We can abandon old, unworkable behavioral patterns or habits and replace them with workable ones. We can resolve inner conflicts and extinguish negative residue of any origin. We can overcome growth barriers and subdue the self-defeating mechanisms of parasitic vampirism. The Corridor of Power is structured to achieve each of these important goals. Here's the procedure.

Step 1. **Peaceful Imagery.** Find a comfortable, quiet place and with your eyes closed, generate a mental picture of a particularly peaceful scene. Examples are a blue sky with white, billowy clouds; a calm sea with a ship on the horizon; a still lake at sunset with waterfowl in the distance; and a tree silhouetted against a brilliant sunset—to mention but a few of the possibilities. Take plenty of time for the picture to form clearly in your mind.

Step 2. **Corridor of Power.** Turn your thoughts inward and envision your innermost being as a wide corridor with areas of both light and shadow. Think of the light as enlightenment and the shadows as either undeveloped potential or inhibitors to growth, such as conflicts, fears, and so forth. Notice doors on each side of the corridor, and think of them as gateways to new growth and enlightenment. Picture each door as having a radiant color, with each color representing certain specialized growth resources. Think of yellow as representing mental growth and development, blue as representing serenity and well-being, green as representing healing and balance, violet as represent spiritual strength and enlightenment, pink as representing motivation and success, and orange as representing inner awareness and self-realization. At this point, you can envision other doors of color to represent other growth resources. Picture at the end of the corridor a glowing white door to represent the limitless resources of the higher cosmos.

Step 3. Doors of Growth. Envision yourself entering the inner corridor of your being with its light, shadows, and doors on either side. Spontaneously select a door of color that appeals to you, open it, and allow abundant new growth energies as a luminous mist to flow into the corridor, illuminating it with bright, new color. Let all shadows and darkness disappear as bright, luminous color permeates the corridor. Open other doors of color at will, and let their energies flow into the corridor, illuminating and infusing your innermost being with new energy.

Step 4. The Cosmic Door. Turn your attention to the radiant white door at the end of the corridor, and sense yourself being drawn toward it. Upon reaching the door, open it and let the flow of bright cosmic light fill the corridor with new energy in its purest form. Allow the flow of cosmic energy to continue until the corridor of your total being is fully saturated with bright cosmic energy.

Step 5. Affirmation. The corridor of your being now energized and filled with cosmic light, you are ready to leave the corridor by turning your attention to the peaceful scene you envisioned at the beginning of this procedure. Affirm: *I am now empowered to reach new levels of growth and fulfillment. I have all the resources required to achieve my highest goals.*

Step 6. Triangle of Power. Erect a triangle with your hands by joining the tips of your thumbs to form the triangle's base and the tips of your index fingers to form its apex. Think of the three sides of the triangle as representing the three components of your being—mind, body, and spirit. Affirm: *Mentally, physically, and spiritually, I am now fully empowered, balanced, and attuned. Nothing can defeat me in my quest for growth and greatness.*

You can use the Triangle of Power as a post-procedure gesture at any time to reactivate the empowering effects of the full procedure. The full procedure should be practiced periodically, however, to reinforce its effectiveness and to discover new dimensions of growth potential, both within yourself and the higher cosmos.

Energy Replacement Strategy

The Energy Replacement Strategy was originally developed in our laboratories in an effort to extinguish parasitic phobias. In use, however, it was found to be equally effective in the treatment of other parasitic anxieties, including obsessive and compulsive reactions. Although the procedure focuses primarily on sensory experience, it indirectly addresses the underlying conditions that give rise to parasitic vampirism. It uses strategies that redirect attention away from the parasitic symptoms and focuses awareness on designated sensations. Rather than denying the unpleasant symptom, the procedure finds a pleasant substitute for it. From a neurological perspective, the procedure blocks certain neural pathways and short-circuits the neural firings that activate the anxiety reaction. A major goal of the procedure is to deprive parasitic vampirism of the energy required for expression. With repeated use of the procedure, the parasitic reaction, whether phobia, obsession, compulsion, or other anxiety condition, eventually becomes like a plant without water—it withers and dies. Here's the procedure.

Step 1. Sensory Focusing. Momentarily focus your attention on your sensory responses—sight, smell, taste, touch, and hearing.

Step 2. **Controlled Vision.** First, view your physical surroundings, noting such characteristics as color, shape, movement, and so forth. Then, while facing forward and without shifting your focus, expand your peripheral vision to its limits. Notice for a few moments the left limits of your peripheral vision without shifting your forward focus; then notice for a few moments the right limits of your peripheral vision, again without shifting your forward focus. Finally, let your vision return to normal as you notice the wondrous sense of well-being and stillness within. Give yourself permission to experience that inner quietness to its fullest.

Step 3. **Circular Touch.** Bring the palms of your hands together and gently rub them against each other as you sense warm energy building between them. Separate your palms and use the tip of your right index finger to slowly form a circle in the palm of your left hand. Envision the circle and note the silken sensation as you slowly trace the circle several times with the tip of your right finger. Continue to trace the circle as you affirm: *I am now in full command of my life. I am energized, protected, and secure. I am fully empowered.*

Step 4. **Empowerment Cue.** Affirm in your own words your power to use Circular Touch (Step 3) at any time as a cue to instantly activate the empowering effects of the full procedure.

The convenient, inconspicuous circular touch cue can be used at will as a powerful energizing and protection strategy. It can instantly extinguish fear associated with heights, closed or narrow spaces, darkness, bridges, and social situations, to list but a few. It can interrupt the thought processes and eliminate the behaviors associate with a wide range of obsessive-compulsive conditions. Aside from these applications, the procedure is highly effective in managing stress and promoting a general state of personal well-being.

Summary

We now know that psychic vampirism exists in a variety of forms. In this chapter, we examined parasitic vampirism, a widespread internal condition in which the person is driven by vampire-like forces that not only consume internal energy resources but also assert a wear-and-tear effect on the energy system.

Parasitic vampirism is psychic vampirism in one of its most disquieting forms. Like a parasite, it attaches itself to the inner self and drains it of the vital resources required for daily functioning. If allowed to run its course, this menacing form of vampirism can lead to a total breakdown of the internal energy system. With the energy system rendered nonfunctional, victims of parasitic vampirism often turn to one-on-one psychic vampirism in a desperate effort to meet their energy needs.

An array of negative self factors, including a poor self-image, insecurity, frustration, feelings of inferiority, and hopelessness, is often the catalyst that gives rise to parasitic vampirism. Early developmental factors as well as past-life experiences are often contributing factors. Active parasitic vampirism can involve phobias, obsessions, compulsions, and a wide range of other anxiety-related conditions, which generate a vicious inner cycle with seemingly a life of its own.

Fortunately, procedures are now available to counteract parasitic vampirism and break its vicious cycle. As we have seen, intervention strategies have been developed to overpower parasitic vampirism by repairing and unlocking old energy channels and opening new ones as well as counteracting the behavioral manifestations of the phenomenon. The results are a rejuvenated, energized system that is functional and fully empowered.

SEVEN

Psychic Vampirism and Altered States

ALTERED STATES OF consciousness can include any state that differs markedly from the ordinary state of mental awareness. Common examples are sleep and dreaming, hypnosis, astral projection, and various meditative and mystical states.

Altered states of consciousness are relevant to our study of psychic vampirism for several reasons. Although certain altered states could conceivably increase one's vulnerability to vampire influences, they can, when appropriately incorporated into relevant strategies, fortify our energy system and increase its power to repel any assault against it. Beyond that, when appropriately applied, altered states can enrich our lives with new meaning, success, and power. Certain altered states are, in fact, among the most effective techniques known for promoting mental, physical, and spiritual well-being. They can connect us to the innermost part of ourselves, and attune us to the highest cosmic source of unlimited power.

In this chapter, we will examine three altered states—sleep, hypnosis, and astral projection—with emphasis on the relevance of each state to psychic vampirism. We will offer specific step-by-step procedures that incorporate altered states as effective growth strategies with power to combat psychic vampirism. While focusing on vampire-related applications, we will examine the relevance of each altered state to other personal empowerment goals.

The Relevance of Sleep

According to Shakespeare, "We are such stuff as dreams are made on, and our little life is rounded with a sleep!" Since about a third of life is spent in sleep, understanding the relevance of that important state is essential to our personal empowerment, including our capacity to ward off psychic vampirism.

Because our psychic defenses during sleep tend to be relaxed, the possibility of a psychic vampire attack while sleeping could significantly increase. Suddenly awakening with either pounding heart or inability to move is an indication that a vampire attack could be underway; whereas awakening with shortness of breath, lightheadedness, dizziness, and weakness are symptoms of a very recent vampire attack. Since the amount of energy lost due to a vampire attack during sleep can be critical, acquiring appropriate protection and intervention skills applicable to sleep is, therefore, essential.

Fortunately, the sleep state is highly receptive to our intervention efforts. Prior to sleep, we can program the sleep process to automatically resist any threat of psychic vampirism. We can fortify the internal energy system and mobilize its potential to turn back any attempted vampire assault during sleep. Upon awakening, we can call forth our inner resources to protect us from vampirism throughout our waking hours.

The Dream State

On average, the eight-hour sleep period consists of four or five dream periods with the duration of dreams successively increasing from around ten minutes to approximately fifty minutes. Typically laden with symbolism, dreams function to protect sleep while simultaneously conveying important messages to conscious awareness. Simply contemplating a problem situation immediately before falling asleep, for instance, can stimulate dream mechanisms to produce a quality solution. Also, reviewing personal goals immediately before falling asleep can generate motivational dreams that build self-confidence and positive expectations of success.

Since the subconscious is a complex repository of knowledge and power, understanding our dreams as subconscious messengers is not always easy. Nevertheless, certain dreams, while laden with symbolism, do seem to be directly related to psychic vampirism. They often use compelling strategies to warn of an impending vampire attack and implore action. In extremely urgent situations, the dream can be so intense that it interrupts sleep in an effort to prevent a vampire attack or, when the attack is already underway, to promptly end it. Unfortunately, simply interrupting sleep may not effectively counteract the attack; deliberate intervention upon awakening may still be required to either prevent or end the attack.

Among the more obvious dream messages that warn of an impending vampire attack are images of a dark, sometimes grotesque figure hovering over the body, snake-like tentacles thrashing out from the darkness, and threats of an attack by either persons or animals. Here are other examples of dream contents that hold particular relevance to psychic vampirism.

A stalled vehicle or brake failure while driving. Failed efforts to escape an impending vampire attack.

Caught in a web. Victimized by either parasitic vampirism or ongoing one-on-one vampirism.

Seriously injured, particularly stabbed or cut. A severe vampire attack with possible long-term damage to the energy system.

Attacked by monsters. Victimized by group psychic vampirism.

A dangerous situation, such as a near-accident. A social relationship with potential for psychic vampirism.

Escape maneuvers, such as running, climbing, and hiding. Efforts to escape entrapment or other involvement in a psychic vampire situation.

Stumbling or falling, particularly into darkness. Victimized by either parasitic or long-term one-on-one vampirism.

Being borne aloft or suspended over terrain. Possibly astral projection or else a desire to escape a threatening situation, including psychic vampirism.

Trapped in a crawlspace or a narrow corridor. Either parasitic vampirism of the phobic type or else resistance to viable growth options.

An aggressive attack on another person. One-on-one vampirism in which the dreamer assumes the vampire role.

Loss of control, such as in steering a vehicle. An entangled relationship with the possibility of victimization by a psychic vampire partner or associate.

Difficulty completing an important task. Failure in coping with the threat of psychic vampirism in its various forms.

Being subdued by a person who has harmed or betrayed you. Overwhelming feelings of vulnerability resulting from failed attempts to resist recurring psychic vampire assaults.

Dreams of color in which creative ideas and solutions emerge. Cosmic balance and protection from psychic vampirism.

Recurring dreams with any of these contents are particularly significant. Unfortunately, many of our dream experiences are soon lost to conscious awareness. Like pebbles tossed into a pool, they sink rapidly into the subconscious almost immediately after dreaming. You can, however, retrieve many of your dream experiences by simply keeping a dream journal. By making written daily entries immediately upon awakening, and then reflecting upon the dream experience, you can often discover the dream's hidden messages, including those related to psychic vampirism. Given insight into the meaning of your dreams, you can discover the bountiful resources of your subconscious and more effectively use them to enrich your life.

Sleep Protection Procedure

The empowerment potential of sleep was recognized as early as 500 B.C. by Heraclitus, who noted, "Even sleepers are workers and collaborators in what goes on in the universe." At a more personal level, Baltasar Grecian wisely noted in A.D. 1647 that "it is better to sleep on things beforehand than lie awake about them afterward."

Aside from its primary role of meeting a basic physiological need, sleep offers a host of empowerment possibilities. It provides a critical incubation period required for solving many complex problems and spawning new ideas. Many important inventions and scientific breakthroughs were the products of sleep and dreaming that generated relevant insight and, in some instances, highly innovative technical designs. The dream state is especially conducive to extrasensory awareness, particularly precognition in which dream images of crucial future events emerge.

The Sleep Protection Procedure recognizes the many spontaneous empowerment functions of sleep as well as our capacity to activate new functions through deliberately intervening into the sleep experience. The procedure uses the brief transitional, trace-like state that immediately precedes sleep along with the normal waking process to fortify the energy system and protect it from psychic vampirism. It recognizes our abundant subconscious resources and places them in a state of readiness to repel any attempted invasion of psychic vampirism during sleep. Equally important, the procedure is highly effective in promoting peaceful, rejuvenating sleep and dreaming, even with very limited practice. Here is the procedure.

Step 1. Pre-sleep Imagery. Immediately before falling asleep, clear your mind of all thoughts and allow peaceful images to spontaneously flow in and out of your mind. Select a particularly pleasant image, perhaps a nature scene such as a landscape at sunset, a waterfowl in flight, or a sail by moonlight. Take a few moments to focus your full attention on the image, noting such details as color, shape, and motion. Give special attention to the serenity the image evokes.

Step 2. Goal Formulation. As you become increasingly drowsy, shift your attention to your solar plexus region as the center of your internal energy system. Sense that energy center at the core of your innermost being. Sense the vibrant energy emanating from that center infusing your body and enveloping your total being with a powerful, protective shield. Affirm in your own words that as you sleep, you will be protected and secure from any threat of psychic vampirism. Visualize your subconscious as a vast region of inner light with power to repel instantly the dark forces of vampirism. Affirm that any attempted vampire invasion will be decisively met with radiant, luminous energy that will promptly drive it back. At this point, you may wish to formulate other goals and affirm your ability and intent to achieve them.

Step 3. Cosmic Protection. Sense your connection to the bright center of the cosmos; and affirm in your own words that, as you sleep, the highest powers of the cosmos will be your constant protection. Envision bright energy of cosmic origin melding with your own energies to fully saturate and energize you mentally, physically, and spiritually.

Step 4. Sleep. Shift your attention to the scene you visualized in Step 1, noting again such details as color, shape, and motion. Continue to focus on the scene until sleep ensues, typically within a few minutes.

Step 5. Awakening Empowerment. Upon awakening from sleep, sense again bright cosmic energy from the center of the cosmos melding with your own energy system to protect and empower you totally. Affirm: *I am energized, attuned, and balanced. I am at one with the cosmic source of pure energy. I am safe, secure, and protected. I am empowered to achieve my highest goals.*

This procedure, while specifically structured to protect the energy system and prevent the depletion of energy associated with psychic vampirism, is equally effective when applied to other personal empowerment goals. Step 2 can be easily modified to include such objectives as slowing the aging process, promoting wellness, increasing creativity, improving memory and concentration, and ensuring career success, to mention only a few of the possibilities. For long-term effectiveness, the procedure should be practiced at least twice weekly.

Aside from sleep protection, I have personally used the Sleep Protection Procedure to accelerate learning of a new language, and to ensure success of several important business ventures. I have also found the procedure to be particularly effective in promoting health and fitness. Along a totally different line, a talented drama student used the procedure to improve his acting skills. He asserts, "The procedure helped me to become more self-confident and to fine-tune my performance." Another student used the procedure to get into a particular graduate program. Now in the job of her choice, she recalls, "The procedure helped me to clarify my goals, and to literally transform them into realities."

The Role of Hypnosis

Hypnosis is a trance state in which receptivity to suggestion is increased. As an altered state of consciousness, hypnosis exists on a continuum ranging from a very mild state of increased receptivity to a very profound, sleep-like state sometimes called the somnambulate level. Although anyone can be hypnotized, the degree of susceptibility varies from person to person. Motivation along with the ability to concentrate and form mental images facilitates the trance state. A firm intent to enter the trance state is critical to both the induction process and success in achieving the desired outcomes of the trance experience.

For most personal empowerment applications, including goals related to psychic vampirism, self-hypnosis is preferred over hypnosis induced by a trained hypnotist. When self-induced, the trance state remains under the full control of the hypnotized subject. While the procedures differ for self-hypnosis, all hypnosis can be seen as self-hypnosis in that without a receptive subject, the trance state will not occur.

For any given application, the preferred level of hypnosis depends on the nature of the stated objective. I have found that a mild to moderate trance state is sufficient for most self-improvement purposes; however, a deeper level is required for certain goals, including past-life and age regression as well as deeper probes of the subconscious. In most instances, the deep trance state requires appropriate safeguards, which are usually incorporated into the induction procedure. We will later present detailed self-induction strategies along with effective deepening techniques that can be used with ease and very little practice to achieve the desired level of hypnosis.

Hypnosis recognizes the vast power of the subconscious as the reservoir of all our past experiences not presently available to conscious awareness. We are the totality of our experiences, including our past lifetimes along with our existence in the discarnate realm between lives. Even when out of reach of consciousness, our past continues to influence our present, including our personal strivings, interests, and achievements. Through self-hypnosis, we can discover our personal past and its relevance to our personal growth. We can enrich our lives with new insight and power to overcome any force that could thwart our growth. We can retrieve those past-life experience that are important to us in the present, including those experiences that relate to psychic vampirism in its several forms. When unknown to us, unresolved past-life issues and painful karmic baggage can haunt us and in some instances slow our progress; but once we become aware of them, they can motivate us to resolve them, and thus learn and grow from them.

Aside from a storehouse of past experiences and accomplishments, the subconscious is a powerful repository of undeveloped potential. Self-hypnosis is one of the most powerful tools known for uncovering our subconscious resources and activating them to achieve our personal goals, including those related to psychic vampirism. Through self-hypnosis, we can tap into that vast region and discover new possibilities for growth and self-fulfillment. As we will later see, we can use self-hypnosis to fortify our internal energy system, activate our vampire defense powers, and energize a new upward spiral of personal growth.

Further reflecting the potential power of hypnosis is a strong body of evidence suggesting that hypnosis can instantly produce totally new, highly developed skills, a phenomenon known as *hypno-production*. Examples are immediate fluency in a new language or sudden advancement in such fields as science and math. I have personally witnessed that amazing function of hypnosis in action.

While in the past-life regressed state, a student with no training in the opera recited verbatim certain passages from Beethoven's opera, *Fidelio,* in German, a language she had not studied. As the regressed state continued, she identified herself as Lilli Lehmann, a German soprano who was born in 1848 and won acclaim on both the operatic and concert stage. In another striking example of hypno-production, a premed student demonstrated during past-life regression an unusual combination of knowledge in four apparently unrelated fields—blacksmithing, medicine, the military, and botany. Speaking in a mixture of French and English, he identified himself as Noel Nicholas, but provided little other personal information during the trance state.

After the session, our follow-up research found that Noel Nicholas, born in 1746, was a French physician who had, incredibly, apprenticed to a blacksmith. After serving as a military surgeon in both France and the United States, he retired in 1795 to found a botanic garden in Reims, thus explaining the student's remarkable command of knowledge in the four separate areas during regression. Furthermore, the regression experience helped to explain his present-life interest in medicine—an apparent carry-over from a past life. In view of the amazing power of the trance state to retrieve knowledge out of the distant past, it is not surprising that hypnosis has steadily gained acceptance as one of the most effective personal empowerment strategies, to include its usefulness in psychic protection.

Psychic vampirism almost always involves subconscious processes. Through self-hypnosis, we can probe the subconscious and uncover those hidden factors that are relevant to psychic vampirism. For instance, self-hypnosis can identify subconscious conflicts and repressed experiences that consume our energies and overwork our energy system, thus increasing our vulnerability to psychic vampirism. The resultant enlightenment is often sufficient to increase our power to ward off psychic vampirism in whatever its form. Self-enlightenment is, in fact, among our most powerful anti-vampire resources.

The potentially empowering effects of self-hypnosis can be extended and enriched through post-hypnotic suggestion. A simple post-hypnotic cue—a slight gesture, image, or thought—presented during hypnosis can be used later to instantly activate the full effects of the trance experience. For instance, such post-hypnotic cues as simply lifting one's toe or touching one's temple can be used to immediately activate our subconscious defenses, erect a protective force field around ourselves, and unleash a new supply of vampire repellent energy.

Since psychic vampire attacks can occur without warning, serious loss of energy and even damage to the energy system can occur before we are aware that an attack is underway. Having in place a subconscious defense system with power to automatically repel an unexpected attack can provide continuing protection against psychic vampirism. Fortunately, such a system exists. Centered in the subconscious, it consists of powerful protective and coping mechanisms designed to work in our behalf. Although the system functions to some degree spontaneously, it is receptive to our conscious intervention. Through self-hypnosis, we can strengthen the system and place its mechanisms in a heightened state of readiness to ensure continuous, effective protection against psychic vampirism. Our subconscious empowerment resources are always enriched when we become consciously aware of them. They become even more powerful when we become their conscious partners and collaborators.

Hypno-liberation and Protection Procedure

The Hypno-liberation and Protection Procedure uses self-hypnosis to unleash our subconscious growth resources, with emphasis on functions that protect and defend us against psychic vampirism. This comprehensive procedure recognizes the various forms of psychic vampirism—including one-on-one, group, and parasitic—as widespread phenomena that all too often thwart our growth and interrupt our progress. By the same token, it recognizes our ability to confront psychic vampirism and reverse its disempowering effects. It emphasizes the capacity of hypnosis to probe the vast, subconscious regions of the mind and uncover new insight and growth possibilities. Through past-life imagery—a highly permissive form of regression—it brings relevant past-life experience into the present and integrates them into a comprehensive growth spiral that knows no limits. It organizes our resources, both conscious and subconscious, into a powerful structure that is more than sufficient to defeat psychic vampirism or any other threat to our well-being.

Developed in our laboratory, the procedure uses a cutting-edge self-induction procedure known as the EM/RC technique that combines eye movement and reverse counting. Although designed primarily to combat psychic vampirism in its various forms, the procedure is flexible and can be adapted to meet almost any self-empowerment need. The full procedure requires approximately one hour during which there must be absolutely no distractions. Here is the procedure.

> **Step 1. Goal Statement.** Begin the procedure by settling back into a comfortable, relaxed position with hands resting to your sides and legs uncrossed so as not to cut off circulation. Take a few moments to clearly formulate your empowerment goals, focusing particularly on those related to psychic vampirism. Examples include (1) empowering your

energy system to confront and defeat psychic vampirism, (2) discovering important insight, including past-life experiences relevant to psychic vampirism, and (3) initiating a powerful upward growth spiral. Specifically state your goals and affirm your intent to achieve them. Use imagery whenever possible to give substance to your stated goals.

Step 2. Eye Movement/Reverse Counting (EM/RC) Trance Induction Strategy. As you become increasingly comfortable and relaxed, close your eyes and give yourself permission to enter the trance state. Visualize yourself enveloped in a powerful sphere of bright energy as you affirm: *I am protected and secure as I now prepare to enter the trance state. Throughout this experience, I will be guided by my higher self and the higher cosmos.* With your eyes remaining closed, further affirm: *By counting slowly backward from 20 while moving my eyes from side-to-side with each count, I will go deeper and deeper into hypnosis. I will remain in full control throughout the trance experience. I can exit hypnosis at any time by simply deciding to do so.* With your eyes still closed, begin the trance by moving your eyes (without turning your head), first to your left on the count of 20, then to your right on the count of 19, then again to your left on the count of 18, and so forth. Accompany each side-to-side eye movement with a reverse count until you reach the count of 1. Upon the count of 1, let your eyes return to normal. Should you reach the desired trance state before the count of one, discontinue the count and proceed to the next step.

Step 3. Deepening the Trance. You can deepen the trance as needed through any of the following procedures: (1) slowly counting again in reverse while interspersing suggestions of drowsiness and depth; (2) using suggestions to induce and then remove sensations such as numbness or tingling at selected body areas, including the hand or finger; and (3) using imagery of a peaceful nature scene, such as a tranquil lake, beach, or meadow, accompanied by suggestions of relaxation and drowsiness.

Step 4. Empowerment Applications. As you remain in the trance state, affirm your intent to experience the expansive domain of your subconscious with its wealth of resources. Visualize your conscious presence in that vast region as bright energy. As your experience that spacious part of yourself, let images and impressions unfold, a process that, at first, may seem similar to the dream experience. Affirm that the emerging experiences are an integral part of your being; and, as such, they are relevant to your present goals.

Step 5. Past-life Imagery. Remind yourself that your past-life experiences are relevant to your present growth, and give permission for them to gently unfold before you as clear images. Should a dark or threatening image emerge, illuminate it with the brightness of your presence rather than attempting to banish it. Think of each image as a source of knowledge and enlightenment, and allow it to become integrated into your total being. Affirm: *I am totally attuned and balanced to the subconscious part of my being.*

Step 6. Psychic Protection and Other Goals. Probe areas of subconscious darkness and illuminate them with bright energy. Illuminate any area of dark residue—including phobias and other anxiety states that feed on your energies—and let them become sources of insight and understanding rather than weights that impede your progress. Form bright images of your goals and let them become registered in your subconscious. For protection from psychic vampirism or any other threat to your well-being, visualize luminous energy permeating the deepest regions of your being and radiating outward to envelop you totally with a shield of bright energy. For other goals, visualize them in as much detail as possible and affirm them as your personal destiny.

Step 7. Post-hypnotic Cue. Bring your hands together as a gesture to symbolize protection, attunement, and balance. Affirm that by simply bringing your hands together, you can at any moment activate the full empowerment effects of the trance experience.

Step 8. Conclusion. Exit hypnosis by counting forward from 1 to 5, with interspersed suggestions of becoming alert and awake. Upon the count of 5, open your eyes and take a few moments to reflect on the trance experience.

Vivid images of past-life experiences often surface in Step 5 of this procedure. They can occur as either instant flashbacks or highly detailed, unfolding images and impressions of past events. Whatever the nature of the manifestation, the resultant catharsis and enlightenment can be profound. In a remarkable instance of the procedure's therapeutic power, an engineer discovered the past-life source of his parasitic insomnia which, for years, had drained him of energy and affected his job performance. In Step 5 of the procedure, he experienced impressions of a distant past life, including vivid images of himself falling asleep while on lookout duty at his mountain post. Awakened by an enemy attack on his village below, he witnessed in horror from his overlook the total annihilation of his tribe. The regression experience revealed the subconscious source of his insomnia—i.e., falling asleep at his post of duty in a past life—and enabled him to resolved the guilt associated with it. Enlightened by the experience, he promptly overcame his insomnia and reversed its debilitating effects on his life.

Astral Projection

Astral projection, also known as out-of-body experience (OBE), astral travel, or soul travel, is the experience of being in a spatial location outside the physical body with conscious awareness intact. As an altered state, astral projection is based on the duality concept of human nature. It recognizes the existence of an astral or extrabiological body with the capacity to disengage the physical body and link awareness to spatial realities independently of physiology.

As a manifestation of the physical body's nonbiological or etheric double, astral projection—perhaps more than any other human experience—provides clear and convincing evidence of survival of conscious identity and awareness after bodily death. As an indestructible energy entity, the astral body in the projected state remains connected to the physical body by a life-support system sometimes called the silver cord. Only at death is the cord severed, whereupon the astral body is liberated to experience in its fullness the discarnate state of continued growth. (As a footnote, this perspective finds interesting confirmation in a Biblical reference which asserts that the silver cord, when "loosed," releases the physical body to return to dust and the spirit to return to God who gave it. Ecclesiastes 11: 6 –7.) Death, from this perspective, is simply a portal to another rich dimension in which consciousness remains intact. In fact, reports of astral experiences, including the near-death experience (NDE), suggest that consciousness not only continues in the astral realm, it is at once sharpened and enriched with new enlightenment and understanding.

Astral projection, whether spontaneous or voluntarily induced, removes the physical limitations of awareness and liberates us to experience distance realities in a very direct and pronounced manner. At a very elemental level, we can travel in astral form to other geographical locations, including remote regions of the globe, and interact with others at great spatial distances. There is some evidence to suggest that we can travel out of body to visit distant planets and other star systems.

Since astral projection is essentially an extrabiological phenomenon, it should come as no great surprise that the spiritual dimension is especially receptive to our out-of-body probes. In fact, out-of-body interactions with that dimension are so common that astral projection is sometimes called the "majestic road" to the spiritual realm. Through astral projection, we can interact with that side of reality and literally experience it as our future destination. Equally as profound, we can discover spiritual guides and growth specialists from the other side who are ready and willing to enrich our lives in the here and now with new insight and power.

Although astral projection can be voluntarily induced through step-by-step procedures, many of our out-of-body experiences occur spontaneously, thus without effort on our part. Among the common examples are "dream experiences" of flying or floating effortlessly in midair and vividly viewing terrain from above. The "lucid dream" in particular seems to have unmistakable elements of astral projection.

Hypnosis and certain meditative states with their accompanying changes in physiology seem to be especially conducive to spontaneous astral travel. Sensations such as slipping out of the body, being carried by an energy current, and drifting freely in space often accompany these altered states. A student participant in our ongoing hypnosis research consistently experienced out-of-body travel that she described as "sailing over the moon and among the stars" during the deeper levels of hypnosis. She described in great detail other planets as seen from a distance during her out-of-body excursions.

Along another line, spontaneous astral projection often occurs during dangerous accident or near-accident situations, with the unfolding event often viewed remotely and sometimes perceived in slow motion. This was illustrated by a law student who sustained serious injuries in an auto crash. Upon impact, he left his body and viewed the accident scene from above, during which he experienced no pain or discomfort. By his report, he was joined during the brief out-of-body experience by a guiding presence that remained with him throughout his recovery period of several weeks. His interaction with the comforting presence, he believed, accelerated his full recovery.

Accounts of the near-death experience often include astral travel, not infrequently with the accompanying presence of a spirit guide or guardian angel. During these profound experiences, highly meaningful interactions with relatives or friends who have crossed over to the other side are common. Through out-of-body visitations to the discarnate realm, we can glimpse the unparalleled growth opportunities that await us when we finally exit this dimension and cross over to that bright side.

Astral projection is particularly relevant to psychic vampirism because it introduces totally new dimensions of personal empowerment possibilities. Through astral projection, we can interact with the higher cosmos and tap its abundant resources. In fact, all the empowerment resources of the higher cosmos, including spiritual guides and teachers, are readily available to us through astral travel.

We can experience specialized cosmic planes of power beyond anything we had previously thought or imagined. We can access cosmic energy in its purest form to shield and fully protect us mentally, physically, and spiritually. We can combat and defeat any oppressive force, including the fiercest onslaught of psychic vampirism. With all the power of the cosmos at our command, nothing is beyond our reach.

Astral Cosmic Voyage

The Astral Cosmic Voyage is specifically designed to induce the out-of-body state, and then through astral travel, to access higher cosmic planes of power. The procedure recognizes the critical importance of deliberate intent (or will) of the higher self to disengage the physical and engage the astral. When combined with relevant imagery and empowering affirmation, decisive intent becomes the essential vehicle for astral travel to any destination in the cosmos.

Astral Cosmic Voyage recognizes our capacity as beings of cosmic origin to experience awareness of a distant, unseen destination, and then travel directly to it. Astral travel using this procedure can be instantaneous from point A to point B, or it can take a slow, indirect route. We can experience a distant physical reality, which can range from a particular earth location to another planet in deep space; or we can transcend the physical realm to experience firsthand a cosmic or spiritual dimension of wondrous beauty and limitless power.

Through Astral Cosmic Voyage, we can interact with any of the cosmic dimension's multiple planes, depending on our personal empowerment needs. The color of the cosmic plane provides a convenient index into its specialized powers. Our studies of the human aura found that interacting with a particular cosmic plane energizes the human aura with that plane's special color (and power). Not surprisingly then, following Astral Cosmic Voyage, the aura assumes not only a new radiance, but also a new infusion of the color that characterized the cosmic plane visited during astral travel.

Cosmic planes of purple are particularly relevant to psychic vampirism—they signify not only psychic protection, but spiritual understanding as well. Bathing in the energies of the purple plain fortifies the astral body with protecting power while energizing consciousness with important new insight. Astral travel to this plane is recommended as an energizing activity for individuals as well as groups seeking psychic protection and spiritual strength.

Cosmic planes of green signify mental, physical, and spiritual well-being. The energies of the green plane are particularly effective in repairing damage inflicted upon the energy system by one-on-one psychic vampirism. This plane is also recommended for counteracting parasitic vampirism, particularly parasitic phobias. A college administrator with a history of fear of flying found that bathing in this astral plane prior to a scheduled flight reduced his fear to a level that he could fly in reasonable comfort. With repeated use of Astral Cosmic Voyage, he finally overcame the fear of flying altogether.

Cosmic planes of yellow are associated with wisdom and success. Interacting with the yellow plane and bathing in its energies are especially recommended for those who interact regularly with large numbers of persons. Aside from its effectiveness in repelling psychic vampirism, bathing in the energies of this plane can stimulate intellectual functioning and increase effectiveness in working with others. Many of my students have used this procedure to improve test performance and increase their grade-point average. A former student who won his bid for elected office attributed his success largely to his regular interactions with the yellow plane.

Planes of blue are associated with peace, balance, and attunement. Interacting with the blue plane's energies is recommended for all who travel to the cosmic realm. Regular voyages to this plane dramatically reduce anxiety and improve self-esteem. The energies of this plane are especially effective in counteracting parasitic vampirism and empowering the internal energy system. Repeated voyages to the blue plane can induce a powerful sense of well-being and eventually disarm the parasitic mechanisms that feed on the energy system.

For Astral Cosmic Voyage, selecting a particular plane or combination of planes can be either spontaneous or deliberate, depending on the empowerment objectives. Once planes of color come into view during the astral state, the plane that is brightest or seems to beckon your interaction is the preferred plane for the moment. That first interaction, however, can be enriched through additional interactions with other selected planes. Here is the procedure, which requires a comfortable setting with no distractions or interruptions.

Step 1. Preparation. Settle back and generate a quiet state of well-being by taking in a few deep breaths and clearing your mind of active thought. With your eyes closed, visualize a glowing mist slowly enveloping your body and fully permeating it as your muscles, joints, and tendons become increasingly relaxed. Think of the mist as cosmic energy with power to energize and protect you mentally, physically, and spiritually. Note the wondrous sense of peace and well-being deep within. Affirm your intent to travel out-of-body to the astral realm, and invoke the protection of that dimension. At this point, you may wish to invite a familiar cosmic guide to be your traveling companion for the duration of your astral journey into the higher cosmos.

Step 2. Out-of-body Induction. Begin the out-of-body induction process by mentally affirming your intent to travel out of your body and into the cosmic realm with its bountiful resources and multiples planes of power. Concentrate on the astral part of your being—that part that is designed to survive your transition to the other side. Sense your spiritual essence, and get the feel of moving freely about as though your were separate and free from your body. (Some astral travelers at this point think of themselves as in discarnate form, that is, free from the corporeal body.) At this stage, you can facilitate the out-of-body process through relevant imagery. For instance, you can visualize yourself walking along a forest trail, in and out of the shadows of towering trees. As you note the intricate patchwork of light and shadows on the forest floor, think of the shadows as representing physical reality and the light as representing spiritual reality. Finally emerging from the shadows of the forest and coming into a place of bright light, note your sense of freedom and separation from your physical body resting at a distance. With the forest and its shadows now behind, sense bright astral energy emanating from the higher cosmos fully enveloping you. Sense yourself as if in apparition form, detached from the physical and gently ascending. Allow plenty of time for full out-of-body awareness to unfold; then remind yourself that you can travel at will throughout the cosmos to interact with its various planes and draw power from them.

Step 3. Astral Travel. As you survey the cosmic realm, notice the many planes of color until a particularly bright plane commands your attention. Focus only on that plane, and let yourself be drawn to it. Once within the designated plane, linger there until you are fully bathed in its colorful radiance. Sense the plane's abundant energies merging with your own energy system to forge an enveloping sphere of armor sufficient to protect you from any vampire essence or entity. Let yourself become totally infused with the plane's special power. Once the interaction is complete, give yourself permission to visit other planes and engage their specialized powers. (Note: At this step, almost all astral travelers become aware of a spiritual presence that guides their interactions among the various cosmic planes.)

Step 4. The Return. Once the cosmic interaction is complete, turn your attention to the place of bright light near the forest where your out-of-body journey began. Give yourself permission to return to that place, and from there into the forest with its patchwork of shadows and light. Finally back into the presence of your physical body in its familiar setting, note the emerging sense of astral and physical harmony as you become spontaneously reunited with your body.

Step 5. Conclusion. To conclude the procedure, focus on you breathing as you sense again the wondrous peace and harmony permeating your innermost being. Briefly review your excursion into the higher cosmos, and sense yourself enveloped in the radiant, protective sphere of cosmic energy.

Affirm: *I am enveloped and infused with powerful cosmic energy. I am fully protected and secure. I can repel at will the threat of psychic vampirism by simply envisioning myself enveloped in a protective sphere of bright cosmic energy.*

A major advantage of Astral Cosmic Voyage over other out-of-body procedures is its versatility. Through this procedure, you can experience the expansive empowerment effects of the out-of-body state independent of cosmic travel; but by visiting selected cosmic planes, you can access relevant cosmic resources and focus them on specific needs, which for our purposes here include psychic protection.

Aside from its relevance to psychic vampirism, Astral Cosmic Voyage is an excellent strategy for alleviating depression and building self-confidence. It can effectively reduce stress and reverse its wear-and-tear by promoting a sense of security and well-being. It is also a highly useful strategy for breaking unwanted habits. It is one of the best strategies known for managing chronic pain and promoting healing. Fortunately, the procedure's empowering effects are both immediate and long-term.

In my clinical practice, I routinely use Astral Cosmic Voyage, particularly to guide anxiety patients into the peaceful radiance of the blue plane. My patients often comment that if they can succeed in leaving their body to visit another dimension, they should unquestionably succeed in taking command of any life situation that threatens to overwhelm them. That reasonable observation itself is self-empowering—it produces positive expectations that tend to be self-fulfilling.

While Astral Cosmic Voyage is easily mastered and generally effective, it is important to note that a structured out-of-body induction strategy appropriate for everyone has not yet been forthcoming. As in hypnosis, response styles and susceptibility levels for astral projection differ from person to person. A strategy that works for one individual may not work for all. If you prefer some other out-of-body induction strategy, you may find that you can increase its effectiveness by incorporating into it certain aspects of Astral Cosmic Voyage.

While skeptics have argued for years that out-of-body experiences are either delusional or simply products of a vivid imagination, there is a mountain of evidence to support the phenomenon as a valid altered state in which astral experiences do indeed occur. In our controlled laboratory studies, specific physiological changes—which included pulse rate, EEG patterns, blood pressure, galvanic skin response, and electrophotographic patterns—were noted at the point of astral projection and continued for the duration of the of the out-of-body state. Furthermore, the combination of these changes was unique to the out-of-body state—they occurred in no other altered state of consciousness. Further supporting the validity of astral travel are the documented instances of highly specific out-of-body observations that are otherwise difficult to explain. Among the striking examples is a highly controlled experiment conducted at our laboratory in which experimental subjects traveled out of body to a distant campus building to view a painting they had never before seen. Upon their return to the laboratory, they described in remarkable detail the essential elements in the painting. For further details of that experiment, see my book *Astral Projection and Psychic Empowerment.*

Although astral projection is among the noblest forms of human expression, it can unfortunately be misdirected. For instance, its underlying motives can be questionable, such as invading the privacy of others; or even worse, using astral travel as a strategy to gain power or control over others. A major concern in our study of psychic vampirism was whether the out-of-body state could be used by psychic vampires as an attack vehicle. While the evidence supporting one-on-one psychic vampirism at the astral level is limited, it is conceivable that such phenomena do indeed occur. Many of the advanced psychic vampires in our studies admit being adept at out-of-body travel, and a few admit using it to fulfill their vampire needs.

The evidence is also limited and highly subjective concerning vampire interactions involving discarnates. It would seem probable that psychic vampire lifestyles are not suddenly extinguished simply because of one's transition to the other side. It follows that psychic vampirism between discarnate vampires and incarnate victims—which we could call discarnate-to-incarnate vampirism—could therefore continue, particularly when unevolved, earthbound discarnates are isolated from the cosmic growth resources of the other side. Fortunately, the vampire protection strategies presented in this book are applicable across the board. Whatever the form of vampirism or the nature of the threat and the dimensions involved, we now have the knowledge and power to encounter and defeat it.

While psychic vampire interactions could conceivably occur between incarnate and discarnate dimensions, it is important to note that most of the interactions between these dimensions are not vampire related, but are instead positive and productive. Almost without exception, we are empowered through our interactions with discarnates, and they are, in turn, empowered through their interactions with us. Certain interdimensional strategies have, in fact, been developed to facilitate empowering interactions with the discarnate realm and facilitate the liberation of unevolved discarnates.

For more information on this topic, see *Psychic Empowerment; Astral Projection and Psychic Empowerment;* and *Aura Energy for Health, Healing, and Balance.*

Summary

In this chapter, we examined three critical altered states—sleep, self-hypnosis, and astral projection—with emphasis on the relevance of each to psychic vampirism. Together, these altered states are important to our study of psychic vampirism because they increase our capacity to repel the potentially destructive phenomenon while activating a host of related inner growth potentials. The Sleep Protection Procedure, for instance, can be used to provide protection during the sleep and waking state alike. It is also applicable to a myriad of other personal empowerment goals. Similarly, the Hypno-liberation and Protection Procedure can protect and defend us against psychic vampirism in its various forms while unleashing an abundance of subconscious growth resources. Not infrequently, images of past-life significance emerge during hypnosis with profound catharsis and enlightenment effects. Finally, the Astral Cosmic Voyage is a highly flexible and versatile out-of-body procedure with empowerment possibilities that range from psychic protection to pain management.

Although more study is needed concerning altered states, the evidence at present is clear: The greater our understanding of altered states and their relevance, the greater our understanding of ourselves and the nature of our existence. By mastering the strategies presented in this chapter, we can become more enlightened while enriching the quality of our lives. We can become empowered to achieve our highest goals and reach a new level of personal growth and fulfillment.

EIGHT

Psychic Protection and Empowerment Tools

NUMEROUS TANGIBLE OBJECTS, along with structured procedures that use them, are now available as tools for personal empowerment and protection against psychic vampirism. The use of tangible objects as psychic tools recognizes at least two interesting possibilities. First, the effects of the tool may be due to psychological factors primarily. For instance, our belief in the tool, and the associations we form with it, could generate a powerful expectancy, or placebo effect. As a result, certain latent mental faculties with power to influence the functions of both mind and body could be set into motion. From that view, the tool, being inert, is effective only when we incorporate it into our belief system, whereupon the belief, not the tool, is empowering.

A second possibility emphasizes that certain tangible objects function as empowerment tools because of their intrinsic characteristics. The direct empowering effects of these tools rest in their essential nature or structural properties rather than our perceptions or associations with them. For instance, certain tools, such as the quartz crystal, are often considered energizing because of their ingrained capacity to directly influence the human energy system. But while the sheer presence of these tools can be empowering, we can often program them to achieve highly specific goals, such as balancing, attuning, and protecting the human energy system. Other tools, such as the pyramid, while apparently nonreceptive to human programming, are thought to be either receivers or generators of energy, with power to disperse it. The empowering effects of these tools would depend primarily on their physical presence or proximity to us. They could, therefore, be effective even when we were unaware of them. Yet other tangible tools, among them dowsing rods and the pendulum, are typically seen as sensitive responders to either human influences or certain external conditions. By their responses under appropriately controlled conditions, we could gain important information that would otherwise remain unavailable to us.

My approach in the use of psychic tools incorporates each of the above possibilities, while emphasizing that the effectiveness of any tool can be increased through our interactions with it. Interactions that, in some way, link us to the tool can generate a synergistic effect in which the power of the tool and the power of the mind are both enhanced. Even tools with absolutely no intrinsic power can become a catalyst that activates the mind's powers through appropriate empowerment procedures.

Among the tools noted particularly for their psychic empowerment potential are the quartz crystal, pyramid, and crystal ball. In the discussion that follows, we will explore each of these tools and its relevance to psychic vampirism.

The Quartz Crystal

The quartz crystal is an ideal psychic empowerment tool, primarily because of its unusual receptivity to human programming. There is evidence that the crystal, when appropriately programmed and then either worn or kept in close proximity to the physical body, can empower the human energy system and spontaneously deflect vampire assaults that are directed against it. The crystal is particularly effective in situations involving prolonged exposure to psychic vampirism, such as sometimes found in the work setting.

When appropriately programmed and used, the crystal can generate a protective shield around oneself, thereby rendering any vampire attack effort harmless. Following an attempted vampire attack, the crystal has been known to take on actual structural change, such as a temporary dark fleck or inclusion in its interior region. In that situation, the crystal is seen as "taking a vampire hit," thereby protecting the targeted victim's energy system not only from a loss of energy, but from the possibility of serious damage to the system as well.

The Crystal Protection Procedure

The Crystal Protection Procedure uses the crystal to energize and protect the human energy system. The procedure guides the selection, programming, and application process. It incorporates the crystal into a dynamic interaction that includes both mental and physical components. The procedure can be used for a crystal already in your possession, or for a fresh crystal to be selected from an assortment. Here is the procedure.

Step 1. Crystal Selection. Begin by stating in your own words your goal of using the crystal in your effort to energize and protect your energy system. While reflecting on your stated goal, select a crystal that seems appropriate to your needs. When selecting a crystal from an assortment, slowly pass your hand, palm side down, over the assortment and note the crystal that seems to stand out from the assortment. Briefly hold the crystal in your hand and sense your interaction with it. If the selected crystal seems inappropriate to your needs, return it to the assortment and repeat the selection process until you find a suitable crystal.

Step 2. **Crystal Programming.** Programming the selected crystal is a two-fold process that includes both deprogramming (sometimes called "cleansing") and installing a new program. To deprogram the crystal, simply hold it briefly under cool running water while stroking it gently; and then place it on a towel to air-dry. To install a new program, hold the crystal in your palm as you invite it in your own words to become your empowerment partner, and then affirm your goal: *My goal is to energize and protect my energy system. Together, we will achieve that goal. Our interaction will empower me to neutralize and defeat psychic vampirism in whatever its form or strategy.* (You may at this point program the crystal for other personal goals by simply stating your goals and inviting the crystal to work with you in achieving them; however, a single crystal should be programmed for no more than three goals, preferably each of which is related.) To save the program, simply state: *Please stay.*

Step 3. **Crystal Application.** Once programmed, the crystal usually functions best when in close proximity to the physical body, such as when worn as an ornament or carried in your pocket, briefcase, or purse. You can enrich the crystal's functions by periodically stroking it while affirming your goals. For protection during sleep, the crystal can be situated on a bedside table or dresser.

Aside from its effectiveness in protecting against one-on-one psychic vampirism, the crystal can be a powerful tool when used to combating parasitic vampirism. For that purpose, Step 2 of the above procedure is expanded to include specific goal statements and affirmations related to the parasitic condition, such as phobias, obsessions, compulsions, and generalized anxiety. For treating phobias, the crystal can be programmed to promote a desensitization process and establish new associations that extinguish the phobia and replace it with a calm, peaceful state of well-being. For obsessive-compulsive conditions, the crystal can be programmed to interrupt the disempowering thought-behavior interaction and replace it with totally new thought processes and behaviors. For generalized anxiety, the crystal can be programmed to facilitate relaxation and induce feelings of security and self-confidence. As noted earlier in this book, parasitic vampire conditions are usually developmental in nature—they often extend to childhood; and in some instances, they even reach into past lives. Perhaps not surprisingly, overcoming them requires perseverance and determination. Fortunately, simply stating your goals and affirming in your own words your intent to work together with the crystal as your empowerment partner tends to initiate an empowering interaction that can lead to complete success.

As a psychologist, I found early on in my clinical practice that almost everyone regardless of age and background is receptive to the crystal as an empowerment tool. College students seem to be especially receptive to using the crystal for a wide range of empowerment goals. My approach in using the crystal with students includes first helping them to form relevant goals, and then personally guiding them in selecting, programming, and using the crystal, with the student always at the center of the process.

While applicable to various goals, the programmed crystal has been highly effective in counteracting psychic vampirism. Victims and potential victims of psychic vampirism, as well as psychic vampires themselves, have successfully neutralized vampirism and reversed its effects by protecting and energizing the internal energy system. For each application, the programmed crystal seems to assume more than a supportive role—it actively restores malfunctioning energy mechanisms, attunes the energy system, and unleashes totally new growth energies.

There is considerable evidence to suggest that the crystal, itself an element of nature, can function for longer periods of time and from greater distances when certain other elements of nature are incorporated into the programming process. A former student reported that she programmed crystals regularly for various purposes, but instead of wearing the crystal or keeping it close at hand, she tossed it into a fountain at the center of her herbal garden. She believed the energies of fountain and plants worked together to amplify and help target the crystal's energies. This modified procedure, by her report, helped her to complete an MBA program, pass a professional licensing examination, secure an excellent job, and more recently, meet the love of her life. Along a different line, an imaginative CEO of a highly successful industrial firm reported that he often programmed crystals to help secure contracts and achieve other important company goals. Immediately after programming the crystal, he placed it at the base of the company's flagpole, which he believed served as an antenna to amplify the crystal's power and disperse its programmed energies.

I've found that including a large tree as a supplement to crystal programming seems to increase the crystal's effectiveness, not only for psychic protection but for various other purposes as well. I routinely use crystal programming that incorporates a very old "crystal-friendly" oak tree for psychic protection or when faced with challenging personal situations. My procedure consists first of programming two crystals using the Crystal Protection Procedure; and then, with the first crystal kept close at hand, placing the second crystal slightly underground at the base of the giant tree. Finally, with my hands resting upon the tree's trunk, I invite the tree to amplify and disperse the crystal's energies. I leave the crystal at the tree's base to promote a continuous interaction between the tree and crystal. Over the past twenty years during which I've used this procedure many times, the crystal-tree interaction never failed—it, in fact, often surpassed my highest expectations.

I have found that crystal programming incorporating a tree is especially effective as a group activity. It is useful in motivating groups while organizing group efforts and focusing them on desired goals. For instance, a parapsychology endowment drive conducted by the Parapsychology Foundation at Athens State University in the 1980s saw a dramatic spike in its fundraising results through crystal programming that incorporated a magnificent campus tree believed to be the oldest in the state. Having formulated its fundraising goals, the Foundation's five-member endowment committee programmed two crystals simultaneously to energize its fundraising efforts. The committee then placed one of the programmed crystals a few inches underground against the tree's base, and, with hands resting lightly upon the towering tulip tree, invited it to become a partner in the endowment effort. With one programmed crystal remaining buried at the tree's base, the other crystal was prominently displayed under a glass dome in the Foundation's central office for the duration of the project. As a result of the highly effective drive, the Foundation successfully funded several student scholarships, established a research laboratory, and sponsored scores of laboratory studies, including several mentioned in this book.

Because of its important power role in the Parapsychology Foundation's endowment project, the magnificent campus tree is today known as Hercules. Standing in front of historic Founders Hall from which students observed the Battle of Athens during the Civil War, the stately tree has been used over the years by students and nonstudents alike for a variety of personal goals. Many students have used the tree to gain admission to top-rated graduate programs. A premed student, who had simply placed his hands on the tree and invited it to be his "power partner," gained admission to the medical school of his choice and is today a faculty member at the school. A business administration major attributes his success in the banking industry to crystal programming which incorporated the tree. Alumni often return to the campus for the express purpose of interacting with the towering tree as a source of inspiration and power (see Figure 9, page 188).

As an aside, Founders Hall provides an interesting backdrop for the splendid tulip tree. Built soon after the founding of the university in 1822, the impressive Greek Revival structure is the site of a recurring apparition believed to be that of a Civil War soldier killed in the bloody Battle of Athens. Known as the Night Stalker, the apparition is often seen either at a gable window overlooking the tree or wandering the halls of the historic building.

My current use of crystals as empowerment tools focuses on promoting research and development at the Parapsychology Research Institute, a nonprofit organization located in northern Alabama. For this application, each member of the Institute's board of directors joined in the empowerment effort by programming a crystal and placing it at the base of a large beech tree in an old-growth forest expressly to amplify the crystal's energies and distribute them worldwide.

In summary, it is conceivable that any individual, group, or organization could benefit from procedures that use the crystal as one of nature's most powerful psychic tools. Supplementing the crystal whenever possible with other elements of nature seems to appreciably increase its empowering potential.

The Pyramid

Second only to the crystal as a popular empowerment tool is the pyramid, or to be more exact, a small replica of the Great Pyramid. For empowerment purposes, the pyramid replica can be of any size or material—glass, wood, crystal, marble, and so forth—provided its

FIGURE 9. HISTORIC TULIP TREE, ATHENS STATE UNIVERSITY.

reduced dimensions are proportional to the Great Pyramid. Orienting the pyramid so that one side is aligned to one of the four cardinal points of the compass is believed by some to promote its effectiveness as an empowerment tool. However, once an empowering relationship with the pyramid has been established, changes in the pyramid's orientation—or even relocating the pyramid altogether—do not seem to affect the pyramid's power.

My interest in the pyramid as a psychic tool began at the early age of seven with a brief third-grade classroom introduction to ancient Egypt. With no previous study of the topic, I found that I already possessed in-depth knowledge of Egyptian history and culture. I was intuitively aware of the country's dynasties and architectural feats, including temples partially hewn into cliffs with their embedded halls and sanctuaries. I had highly detailed information concerning the pyramids, including the Great Pyramid and the earlier Step Pyramid of Zoser. I was familiar with ancient Egyptian rituals, including but not limited to those designed to endow statues and pictures of the deceased with life if the body were destroyed, a practice considered critical for the soul's well-being. Incredibly unfolding, like a movie before me, were scenes of myself actively participating in those ancient rituals.

That early experience provided convincing evidence of my personal connection to ancient Egypt, a connection that was confirmed many years later through past-life regression during which I retrieved highly detailed information regarding my past-life experiences in Egypt. The content of the regression accounts were reviewed by several historians—including a university professor whose specialty was Egyptian history—and found to contain no discrepancies.

My long-term interest in Egyptian culture inspired several controlled laboratory studies designed to investigate the relevance of the pyramid model as an empowerment tool. Not unlike the findings of many other researchers, my work validated the empowerment potential of the pyramid. The small pyramid model, with its exact proportions, was found to retain many of the purported powers of the Great Pyramid after which it is patterned. By its sheer presence, the pyramid model was found to be especially effective in energizing and protecting the human energy system, effects that were particularly evident in aura photographs as well as direct viewings of the aura before and after exposure to the pyramid model. Whether a generator of new energy or a channel for cosmic energy of the highest order, the pyramid is clearly a critical force with far-reaching possibilities.

Equally as profound as the pyramid's apparent intrinsic powers is its adjuvant role when incorporated into structured empowerment strategies. The pyramid can be readily integrated into step-by-step procedures design to promote achievement of a seemingly unlimited range of personal goals. Although the pyramid is essentially nonreceptive to programming, it is a supportive, steadfast collaborator in our goal-related strivings. Even if seen as simply an inert object or symbol, the pyramid can be a visible reminder of our commitment and determination to reach designated goals.

The Pyramid Empowerment Procedure

The pyramid is particularly relevant to psychic vampirism because of its unique capacity to energize the internal energy system while linking it to the highest cosmic source of energy. It can be instrumental in protecting us from the external threat of psychic vampirism by erecting a powerful, impenetrable sphere of energy around the body. Because of its powerful effects on one's internal energy system, the pyramid can strengthen the specific coping resources required to counteract parasitic vampirism. When appropriately applied, the pyramid can alleviate anxiety and other conditions that are the primary energizers of parasitic vampirism. The Pyramid Empowerment Procedure is designed to achieve each of these important goals. The procedure as follows requires a quiet, comfortable setting and the physical presence of a pyramid model.

> Step 1. Pyramid Selection. For this procedure, the pyramid can be of any material but must be small enough to be held comfortably in the palm of your hand.

Step 2. Goal Statement. Assume a comfortable seated position, and, with the pyramid resting on its base in the palm of either hand, formulate your goals, stating them as specific outcomes. While the sheer presence of the pyramid can infuse the energy system with new power, specifying your goals promotes an effective interaction with the pyramid, thus enhancing its spontaneous capacities.

Step 3. Energy Infusion. While focusing your attention on the pyramid as it continues to rest in the palm of your hand, sense the warm energies emanating from the pyramid's base. Place your other hand over the pyramid and sense the tingling energies emanating from the pyramid's apex. Allow the energies of the pyramid to spread into both hands and from there, throughout your total body.

Step 4. Cosmic Energy Infusion. While lying down, place the pyramid over the energy center situated at your solar plexus region. With your eyes closed and your hands resting comfortably to your sides, visualize a channel connecting the apex of the pyramid to the bright energy center of the cosmos. Visualize the connective channel glowing with powerful cosmic energy. Allow the luminous cosmic energy entering the pyramid to penetrate your internal energy center, and from there to saturate your total being. Visualize the glow of cosmic energy enveloping you fully.

Step 5. Affirmation. As you continue to sense the flow of cosmic energy within, affirm: *I am infused and enveloped with the glow of cosmic energy. I am fully attuned, balanced, and protected.* In your own words, affirm that your goals as stated in Step 2 are your unfolding destiny.

Step 6. Conclusion. Resume the seated position and, with the pyramid again resting in your palm, place your other hand over the pyramid as in Step 3. As before, note the pyramid's energies permeating first your hands and then your total body. Think of the pyramid as your unfaltering link to the cosmic source of limitless possibilities. Affirm that by simply viewing the pyramid, or in its absence visualizing it, you will become fully empowered to achieve any goal and to repel any threat to your well-being.

Although simply envisioning the pyramid is an effective empowerment cue, keeping the pyramid near at hand and periodically interacting with it are recommended. I customarily carry in my pocket or briefcase a small crystal pyramid that I occasionally clasp in my hands, an inconspicuous gesture that I find highly effective in promoting alertness and concentration. I often display the pyramid at book signings and circulate it at programs to illustrate its energizing effects. Possibly because of its archetypal significance, almost everyone can relate to the pyramid as a potentially empowering tool.

The Crystal Ball

A universal symbol of harmony and enlightenment, the crystal ball is important as both an object of beauty and tool of power. It is relevant to our study of psychic vampirism because it offers yet another alternative for accessing the hidden sources of psychic protection and power.

Simply gazing at the crystal ball, independent of structured procedures, can expand awareness and stimulate a host of mental processes. It can activate our psychic faculties, particularly *precognition* (ESP of future events) and *clairvoyance* (ESP of present realities), thus providing important new insight and solutions to problem situations. A law student, for instance, experienced during gazing a strong precognitive impression of his father being suddenly stricken with serious illness. The following day, his father was hospitalized with a heart attack. Along a totally different line, a college professor during gazing experienced highly detailed clairvoyant images of an unseen lakefront property he was to later purchase. In recognition of its psychic relevance, I routinely incorporate crystal gazing into my seminars designed to develop psychic skills.

The effectiveness of crystal gazing in stimulating our psychic faculties suggest other important empowerment applications, including its usefulness in combating psychic vampirism. Even when practiced independent of step-by-step procedures, crystal gazing is at once relaxing and energizing. But when integrated into a structured approach, its effects are dramatically increased. It can reinforce the internal energy system and link it to the highest cosmic source of energy. The result is an empowered energy system that is fully functional and protected against any threat of psychic vampirism.

Structured crystal gazing is especially useful as a group empowerment exercise. It can activate dormant group powers while uniting the group's energies and directing them toward designated goals. As a group empowerment tool, the crystal ball can function as a visible channel that connects the group to astral planes of cosmic power. Through the crystal ball, the group can access a limitless supply of energy in its most powerful form.

The Orb of Power

The Orb of Power is designed especially for use by groups as a psychic energizing and protection strategy. The procedure can be easily adapted to groups of any size. It is structured firstly, to exercise the collective energies of the group, and secondly, to empower the total group as well as each member individually.

For this procedure, the crystal ball is seen primarily as a facilitative tool. By centering attention on the interior region of the crystal ball, the group blends and harmonizes its energies, which are, in turn, dispersed throughout the group. Like other empowerment strategies we have discussed, the combined action of the group and the coming together of its energies are synergistic—the total energy returned to the group is greater than the sum of the energies contributed independently by each member of the group. Individuals who make up the group are energized and empowered, first by exercising their internal energy system's sending and receiving mechanisms, and second by interacting with the group and contributing to the overall group process.

Rather than fostering conformity, the Orb of Power celebrates individual differences. The highly flexible procedure recognizes the

uniqueness and incomparable worth of each person. Diversity within
the group is considered an empowerment resource. The synergistic
effect of the procedure is markedly increased through differences
among participants in such personal characteristics as achievements,
orientations, cultural backgrounds, lifestyles, and even energy levels.
Every person's potential for success and greatness is the centerpiece
of this highly inclusive procedure.

As a vampire protection strategy, the Orb of Power organizes and
expands the energies of the group to collectively repel psychic vampirism in its various manifestations. Vampire attacks against the
group, whether from within or without, are promptly neutralized by
the powerful energies generated by the procedure. Vampire surfers
are repelled and driven back by the one-way sphere of energy erected
to envelop the group. Through this procedure, group participants
can discover the protective resources required to repel at a personal
level any threat of psychic vampirism. Victims of parasitic vampirism can experience the group support they need to subdue and overcome the internal processes that exhaust their energy resources. The
procedure can replenish lost energy, strengthen the internal energy
system, and break at once the vicious cycle of psychic vampirism.

In a much broader sense, the Orb of Power can be used on a global
scale to empower and enrich the globe. Empowering energy, once
generated, is never lost. It seeks out its target and performs its designated task. Healing the earth, cleaning up the environment, and promoting global harmony are not beyond the power of groups who
collectively focus their energies. Commitment leads to action. When
a sufficient number of individuals around the world commit their
energies to designated global goals, change will occur. The future of
the planet may very well depend on the combined energies of large
numbers of individuals who are dedicated to making the world a
better place for themselves and future generations. The Orb of Power
can help achieve that important goal. Although designed for use by
groups, the procedure can be easily adapted for individual use.

Here is the procedure that requires a crystal ball, preferably with
a bubble in the center to facilitate gazing.

Step 1. The Gazing Set-up. The procedure is appropriate as an energizing and protection strategy for groups of any size or makeup. It can, however, be used for a wide range of other designated goals. For small groups, the crystal ball is usually placed on a table at the center of the group, which is usually seated in a circular arrangement. For large groups, the ball is usually situated at a slightly elevated position in front of the group to facilitate easy gazing. Whatever the size of the group, the crystal ball should be clearly visible to each participant.

Step 2. Gazing and Visualization Warm-up. The purpose of this step is to exercise the group's gazing and visualization skills. In unison, the group focuses its attention on the interior region of the crystal ball. If the ball has a bubble at its center, attention is focused on the interior of the bubble. Following a few moments of relaxed gazing, group members exercise their visualization skills by closing their eyes and imaging the crystal ball, after which gazing resumes with intermittent visualization.

Step 3. Energy Sending. At this step, the group exercises it energy-sending powers. Together, group members rub their hands briskly together, palm against palm, to generate sensations of energy; and then, with their palms turned facing the crystal ball, they envision in unison bright energy streaming from their hands to envelop the crystal ball with a powerful accumulation of group energy.

Step 4. Cosmic Connection. With hands returned to the relaxed position, the group resumes gazing at the crystal ball for a few moments. Then, with eyes closed, the group visualizes the crystal ball as a glowing replica of the bright energy core of the cosmos. Following a few moments of visualization, gazing is resumed, whereupon a bright glow of powerful energy enveloping the crystal ball will almost always become visible to the total group.

Step 5. Energy Receiving. With hands again turned toward the crystal ball, the group visualizes radiant streams of energy emanating from the crystal ball and flowing into the palms.

At this stage, vibrating sensations in the palms are typical as energy enters them and then flows throughout the body to fully infuse it with a fresh, new supply of energy.

Step 6. Orbs of Energy. With hands relaxed and eyes remaining closed, the group visualizes a glowing orb of protective energy enveloping each group member. The group then collectively visualizes a gleaming orb of energy enveloping the total group.

Step 7. Affirmation of Power. As imagery of the bright personal orbs of energy within the larger collective orb continues, the group affirms the empowering, energizing effects of the procedure. Designated group goals are affirmed, not simply as possibilities but rather as emerging realities. At this step, group members may wish to specify their personal goals and affirm their power to achieve them.

Step 8. Global Empowerment. To empower the globe, the group visualizes the globe and then, with hands again turned outward, disperses energy in all directions to fully infuse it. Specific regions of the globe can be targeted for a special infusion of energy. The group then collectively envisions the globe enveloped and infused with luminous energy.

Step 9. Empowerment Cue. The group collectively affirms its power to activate the full effects of the procedure by simply gazing at the crystal ball, or in the absence of the crystal ball, simply visualizing it.

The above empowerment cue can be used as often as needed; however, the full procedure should be practiced periodically to maximize the effectiveness of the cue.

The Orb of Power can be easily adapted to focus group energies on a selected individual. A member of the group with a pressing need, for instance, could by request become a volunteer recipient of group energy. For this application, the volunteer subject is usually seated either at the center or in front of the group. Group members then send their energies by first rubbing their hands together and then turning them as sending mechanisms toward the receiving subject. Healing and therapeutic energies are particularly receptive to this adapted procedure. After appropriately orienting the group, I often use the procedure in group therapy for the treatment of depression and anxiety with highly positive, long-term results. Also, the procedure has been unusually effective as a motivational and supportive strategy in weight management programs.

Nature's Empowerment Tools

Our natural surroundings are teeming with tangibles which can be used as protection and empowerment tools of the highest order. Our lives can be enriched by simply expanding our awareness of the beauty and magnificence of nature, from our immediate surroundings to the most distant star system. But when we deliberately tap into nature's empowerment resources, we discover possibilities far beyond anything we had imagined or conceived.

The endless empowerment possibilities found in the sights and sounds of nature are especially relevant to psychic vampirism. They connect us not only to that which is around us but also to the innermost part of our being. Beyond that, they connect us to that which lies far beyond the sphere of perceptual reality. Experiencing, for instance, the wondrous serenity of a sunset, the excitement of a summer storm, or the manifold sounds of a meadow elevates the spirit to a new level of insight and understanding of our place in the universe. Given greater awareness of our natural surroundings, we can become more fully balanced and attuned, both inwardly and outwardly.

When we interact with nature, we experience energy in its purest, most powerful form. Our internal energy system becomes revitalized and fully renewed. Faulty functions are restored to their peaks of efficiency; energy systems weakened because of vampire attacks are reinforced and energized; internal parasitic mechanisms that drain our energy resources are disarmed and vanquished; and vulnerable systems become empowered and protected with new psychic defenses. Here are some examples of nature's cosmic tools and ways we can use them.

Trees. Among natures most regal creations, trees function as earth's living antenna to the universe. By simply resting your hands upon a selected tree and affirming it as your connection to the cosmos, you can empower your internal energy system and activate its energizing functions.

Old-growth Forests. Forests are a rich repository of life-force energy. As symbols of permanence and power, old-growth forests are particularly energizing. Energy systems damaged by psychic vampirism are especially receptive to the collective healing energies permeating forests. By merely walking along a forest trail and sensing the forest's blend of power and peace, you can tap into the energy of the forest and the higher cosmos.

The Open Meadow. For many of us, the open meadow with its range of sights and sounds evokes a state of peace and freedom beyond that available from any other source. Its expansiveness is liberating, its sounds are inspiring, and its energies are enlivening. A contemplative walk through a meadow can connect us to both the higher self and the higher cosmos.

Oceans, Lakes, and Streams. The earth's oceans, lakes, and streams manifest the constant flow of life-force energy throughout the universe. By recognizing their enduring power and simply turning the palms of your hands outward toward them, you can experience a new infusion of life-force energy permeating and protecting your total being.

Mountains. The earth's majestic mountains remind us of our potential to rise above the ordinary and reach a higher plane of personal growth and fulfillment. Simply becoming aware of the wonder of their presence is alone a source of inspiration and renewal.

The Universe. Nothing reveals the beauty and magnificence of our existence more than the visible universe with its billions of star systems. And nothing is more empowering than to be attuned to the creative cosmic force that undergirds it.

Summary

Psychic tools are tangible objects with tremendous relevance to our personal empowerment. Whether innately empowering or essentially inert, each tool is a valuable resource with potential to enrich our lives. Among the psychic tools with particular relevance to psychic vampirism are the quartz crystal, pyramid, and crystal ball. Add to these the abundance of tools found in our natural environment and we have a near inexhaustible range of tangibles awaiting our interaction.

Each tool discussed in this chapter is unique in its design and function—the quartz crystal in its receptivity to programming, the pyramid in its direct energizing capacity, the crystal ball in its facilitative role, and nature at large with its limitless range of possibilities. Equipped with the tools of psychic growth and protection, we can be proactive and secure in our efforts to counter psychic vampirism. When appropriately applied, psychic tools provide a coat of armor with power to deflect the darts of psychic vampirism from any source. But beyond that, they help us to achieve an unlimited range of personal goals by connecting us to totally new sources of growth and enlightenment.

NINE

A Seven-Day
Psychic Protection Plan

I HAVE ATTEMPTED throughout this book to strike a workable balance between reasonable concepts and practical application. Both are inextricably linked—they fly to heaven on the same wing. The Seven-Day Psychic Protection Plan translates proven principles into step-by-step procedures that protect against psychic vampirism while promoting personal growth. The plan begins with basic strategies that focus on the internal energy system, and ends with strategies that connect us to the cosmic source of energy in its purest, highest form.

The plan is consistently growth-oriented. It views personal growth not as a destination, but rather as a way to travel. The plan opens the door for new growth, and through growth, greatness. It identifies specific goals related to psychic vampirism, and then presents strategies, some drawn from previous chapters, designed to achieve them. Day one of the plan focuses on ways to promote a functional internal energy system that meets our mental, physical, and spiritual energy needs. On day two, the plan presents two strategies that energize and balance the aura system while protecting it against any intrusive force, including the onslaught of psychic vampirism. On day three, the plan details strategies designed to prevent or counteract parasitic vampirism. Day four examines subconscious growth resources and unleashes them to fortify and protect the internal energy system against psychic vampirism. Day five, a critical point in the plan, introduces astral travel as a vehicle for accessing higher cosmic planes of power. Day six introduces the quartz crystal as a psychic empowerment and protection tool. The final day of the plan focuses on nature and ways of using our natural surroundings as growth and enrichment resources.

The plan is both broad and flexible. You can easily revise it to include other personal goals, or you may wish to supplement it with other procedures found in this book. But whatever your preferred approach, a firm commitment from the start to complete the plan is essential to its success. Once completed, the plan can translate your aspirations into realities. It can initiate within you a totally new spiral of growth and self-fulfillment.

Day One

Goal: To promote a fully functional internal energy system that meets mental, physical, and spiritual energy needs.

Day one of our plan introduces two strategies designed to empower the internal energy system. The Handclasp of Power is designed to repair the damage to the system, revitalize its mechanism, and open up new energy pathways. The Energy Activation Procedure introduces mental and physical techniques that not only enhance the system's functions; they also promote continuous development of the system itself. Both procedures are effective in balancing and attuning the energy system to the higher cosmos.

The Handclasp of Power

Step 1. **Body Scan.** Settle back and while breathing slowly and rhythmically, mentally scan your body from your head downward, briefly pausing at areas of tension. Visualize the tension as a shadowy mist and your conscious presence a luminous glow. Let the glow of consciousness repel the shadowy mist and replace it with bright, new radiant energy. Take plenty of time for the luminous glow of your conscious presence to fully permeate your physical body.

Step 2. Focusing. Focus your conscious awareness on your solar plexus, and think of that region as your energy control center. Visualize your conscious presence at that center as a bright, supercharged force that activates and fortifies your total energy system.

Step 3. Self-infusion. As you remain consciously centered, visualize energy pathways extending outward from your inner control center. You can now identify blocked pathways and open them up to unleash a totally new flow of life-force energy. You can now replace old, nonfunctional pathways with shining, new energy channels. Let the supercharging flow of powerful energy illuminate your total being, inside and out.

Step 4. Cosmic Infusion. Turn your hands upward as you sense radiant beams of pure cosmic energy entering your palms and then spreading inward to bathe and energize every part of your being. Sense vibrant cosmic energy flowing throughout your energy system, saturating it totally with bright cosmic energy.

Step 5. Attunement and Balance. Clasp your hands as a symbol of your oneness with the cosmos. Affirm: *I am now totally balanced and attuned to the higher cosmos.* You can use the handclasp at will as a cue to activate the empowering effects of the full procedure.

You can use the inconspicuous handclasp cue at almost anytime to protect against the invasion of negative forces in any form. It can promote clear thinking and increase your effectiveness and sense of command over the situation at hand. Regular practice of the cue is recommended for the remainder of the seven-day plan.

Energy Activation Procedure

This strategy not only enhances the internal energy system's existing functions; it also promotes continuous development of the system itself.

Step 1. The Energy Center Within. Remind yourself that you are a permanent life-force entity with a powerful energy center deep within yourself. With your eyes closed, visualize that center as the vibrant, luminous core of your being with power to generate and distribute mental, physical, and spiritual growth energy. Think of yourself, along with the energy center within, as a cosmic creation that is constantly evolving.

Step 2. The Power of Consciousness. Focus your conscious awareness on the bright energy core situated in your solar plexus. Let the energies of your conscious awareness gently merge with your internal energy core to activate its powers to generate abundant new energy. Sense the vibrant force of energy building within your solar plexus and slowly radiating new energy into every cell and fiber of your body.

Step 3. Energizing Touch. Place the fingertips of both hand over the energy core at your solar plexus region to further stimulate the balanced flow of revitalizing energy throughout your body. As you hold this touch position, note the tingling sensations in your fingertips, a manifestation of the life-force energy flowing from your central energy system to permeate your total being.

Step 4. Empowerment Affirmation. Affirm: *I am now empowered in mind, body, and spirit. I am energized, protected, and secure. I am empowered to repel psychic vampirism or any other threat to my well-being.* You can add in your own words other specific affirmations related to your personal goals or present life situation.

Step 5. Empowerment Cue. Use the energizing touch gesture as presented in Step 3 at any time to instantly activate the full empowering effects of this procedure.

By regularly practicing this procedure and applying the energizing touch cue whenever needed, victims of psychic vampires discover their power to repel attacks on their energy system; and psychic vampires discover their capacity to generate the energy required to meet their own energy demands, thus making vampirism unnecessary. This procedure is especially recommended for partners in a relationship with a history of psychic vampirism.

Day Two

Goal: To energize and balance the aura system while protecting it against any intrusive force, including the onslaught of psychic vampirism.

Day two introduces two important strategies related to the human aura. The Aura Self-protection Massage is designed to exercise the total aura system and activate its internal defense powers. This procedure jump-starts the aura's inner core, raises the aura's overall energy level, and generates a frequency pattern that effectively repels psychic vampirism, whatever its form. The Finger Interlock Procedure erects a powerful outer shield of radiant energy around the aura while balancing and attuning the aura's internal core to the highest cosmic source of energy.

Aura Self-protection Massage

Step 1. Clockwise Massage. While in a relaxed, seated, or reclining position, with your hands resting comfortably at your sides, take a few moments to visualize the aura enveloping your physical body and the bright, energizing aura core situated in your solar plexus. Place your right hand, palm side down, a few inches above your solar plexus, and begin to massage your aura at that region with small, circular, clockwise movements. Gradually expand the circular aura massage to encompass a larger body region surrounding your solar plexus. Sense the energy swirling in a clockwise direction, first around your solar plexus, then expanding to include your chest and lower abdomen. Following a few moments of clockwise massage, rest your hand to your side as you continue to experience the swirling energy throughout your central body region.

Step 2. Counterclockwise Massage. With your right hand now resting comfortably at your side, place your left hand, palm side down, a few inches above your solar plexus and reverse the clockwise massage to induce counterclockwise motion in the aura. Begin the massage at that region with small, circular, counterclockwise movements. As with the clockwise massage, gradually expand the counterclockwise massage to encompass a larger body region surrounding your solar plexus. Sense the energy swirling in a counterclockwise direction, first around your solar plexus, then expanding to include your chest and lower abdomen. Following a few moments of counterclockwise massage, rest your left hand to your side as you continue to experience the swirling energy throughout your central body region.

Step 3. Repeat Massage. Further exercise the aura system by repeating Steps 1 and 2 above. Throughout the massage, think of your aura's inner core as a powerful generator of energy. Notice the energy building in your central aura region and then spreading throughout your total aura system to envelop your body with a powerful shield of bright, new energy.

Step 4. Balancing and Attuning. To balance and attune the aura's new energies, close your eyes and touch your temples with the fingertips of both hands as you sense vibrant energy permeating your total being.

Step 5. Energizing Affirmation. Affirm in your own words the empowering effects of this exercise. Examples are: *I am fully energized and empowered. The innermost part of my being is now balanced and attuned. I am enveloped in a powerful shield of energy. I am protected and secure.*

Step 6. Energizing Cue. Affirm in your own words your ability to instantly activate the empowering effects of the full procedure by simply closing your eyes and touching your temples with your fingertips as you envision a bright outer shield of energy enveloping your total aura.

Aside from protecting the aura, this procedure is highly useful in repairing damage to the aura inflicted by a psychic vampire attack, even when the specific location of damage to the aura is unknown. With periodic practice of the full procedure, you can use the convenient energizing cue as often as needed to activate the procedure's full empowerment effects.

Finger Interlock Procedure

Step 1. Cognitive Relaxation. Find a comfortable place and take a few moments to mentally relax your body, beginning with the muscles in your forehead and slowly progressing downward. As you scan your body downward, let every fiber and tendon become loose and limp. Envision the tension leaving your body as a mist slowly rising and then vanishing.

Step 2. Finger Interlock. Bring together the thumb and middle finger of each hand to form two circles, then join your hands to form interlocking circles.

Step 3. Affirmation. Hold the finger interlock position as you affirm: *I am totally enveloped with powerful energy. I am balanced within and fully attuned to the higher cosmos. I am protected, secure, and shielded from all harm.*

Step 4. Cosmic Infusion. Relax your hands, and with your palms turned upward envision bright rays of pure energy from the highest cosmos entering your palms and infusing your total being. Affirm: *I am at one with the cosmos. All the power of the universe in now available to me.* Specify your personal goals and affirm your success in achieving them.

Step 5. Finger Interlock Cue. In your own words, affirm that by simply forming the finger interlock as a cue, you can instantly activate the empowerment effects of the full procedure at any time.

You can use the Finger Interlock Cue at will to protect the aura against a psychic vampire attack, or once an attack is underway, to instantly terminate it.

Day Three

Goal: To prevent or counteract parasitic vampirism through acquiring skills that extinguish its symptoms and activate a state of inner empowerment.

Three step-by-step procedures related to parasitic vampirism are introduced for day three. Through the Stress Reduction Response, you can eliminate negative stress, a major symptom of parasitic vampirism, and replaces it with a protected and secure state. Through the Corridor of Power, you can counteract parasitic vampire tendencies and activate your inner growth and protection potentials. Through the Parasitic Replacement Strategy, you can counteract such parasitic anxieties as phobias, obsessions, and compulsions, and replace them with an empowered state of well-being.

The Stress Reduction Response

Step I. **Mental Quietness.** Find a quiet, comfortable place and with your eyes closed, breathe slowly and deeply as you clear your mind of active thought. Turn your thoughts inward, and find a quiet, still place somewhere within yourself. Take plenty of time to search your innermost self until you find that special place. You will know the right place when you find it.

Step 2. **Settling In.** Once you find that inner place of quietness, settle into it, and let yourself become a part of it. Envision your presence in that space as a light form with the capacity to illuminate your total being. Let the brightness of your presence spread slowly throughout your being until you are fully infused with peace and tranquillity.

Step 3. **Physical Relaxation.** From your place of inner quietness, mentally scan your physical body from your head downward.

Pause briefly at any tense area and relax it by taking in a deep breath and then slowly exhaling. Envision the area becoming illuminated with bright energy.

Step 4. Cosmic Balance and Attunement. Sense the cosmic part of your being reaching outward and connecting you to the higher cosmos. Visualize radiant beams emanating from your innermost being and reaching into infinity. Sense yourself becoming balanced with all that exists, from the innermost center of your being to the outermost reaches of the cosmos.

Step 5. Empowerment Affirmations. As you remain in your quiet, inner place, affirm: *I am balanced and attuned to the cosmos. Peace is flowing gently throughout my total being. I am safe, protected, and secure.*

Step 6. Fingertip Engagement. Before opening your eyes, bring your hands together—fingertips against fingertips—as a symbolic gesture of inner peace and power.

This procedure is recommended as a daily exercise for the remainder of the seven-day plan. Following sufficient practice of the full procedure, you can use the simple fingertip engagement gesture at will to generate a relaxed, peaceful state of balance and attunement.

Corridor of Power

Step 1. Peaceful Imagery. Find a comfortable, quiet place, and, with your eyes closed, generate a mental picture of a particularly peaceful scene. Examples are a blue sky with white, billowy clouds; a calm sea with a ship on the horizon; a still lake at sunset with waterfowl in the distance; and a tree silhouetted against a brilliant sunset—to mention but a few of the possibilities. Take plenty of time for the picture to form clearly in your mind.

Step 2. Corridor of Power. Turn your thoughts inward and envision your innermost being as a wide corridor with areas of both light and shadow. Think of the light as enlightenment and the shadows as either undeveloped potential or inhibitors to growth, such as conflicts, fears, and so forth.

Notice doors on each side of the corridor, and think of them as gateways to new growth and enlightenment. Picture each door as having a radiant color, with each color representing certain specialized growth resources. Think of yellow as representing mental growth and development, blue as representing serenity and well-being, green as representing healing and balance, violet as represent spiritual strength and enlightenment, pink as representing motivation and success, and orange as representing inner awareness and self-realization. At this point, you can envision other doors of color to represent other growth resources. Picture at the end of the corridor a glowing white door to represent the limitless resources of the higher cosmos.

Step 3. **Doors of Growth.** Envision yourself entering the inner corridor of your being with its light, shadows, and doors on either side. Spontaneously select a door of color that appeals to you, open it, and allow abundant new growth energies as a luminous mist to flow into the corridor, illuminating it with bright, new color. Let all shadows and darkness disappear as bright, luminous color permeates the corridor. Open other doors of color at will, and let their energies flow into the corridor, illuminating and infusing your innermost being with new energy.

Step 4. **The Cosmic Door.** Turn your attention to the radiant white door at the end of the corridor, and sense yourself being drawn toward it. Upon reaching the door, open it and let the flow of bright cosmic light fill the corridor with new energy in its purest form. Allow the flow of cosmic energy to continue until the corridor of your total being is fully saturated with bright cosmic energy.

Step 5. **Affirmation.** The corridor of your being now energized and filled with cosmic light, you are ready to leave the corridor by turning your attention to the peaceful scene you envisioned at the beginning of this procedure. Affirm: *I am now empowered to reach new levels of growth and fulfillment. I have all the resources required to achieve my highest goals.*

Step 6. Triangle of Power. Erect a triangle with your hands by joining the tips of your thumbs to form the triangle's base and the tips of your index fingers to form its apex. Think of the three sides of the triangle as representing the three components of your being—mind, body, and spirit. Affirm: *Mentally, physically, and spiritually, I am now fully empowered, balanced, and attuned. Nothing can defeat me in my quest for growth and greatness.*

You can use the Triangle of Power as a post-procedure gesture at any time to reactivate the empowering effects of the full procedure.

Energy Replacement Strategy

Step 1. Sensory Focusing. Spend a few moments focusing your attention on your sensory responses—sight, smell, taste, touch, and hearing.

Step 2. Controlled Vision. First, view your physical surroundings, noting such characteristics as color, shape, movement, and so forth. Then, while facing forward and without shifting your focus, expand your peripheral vision to its limits. Notice for a few moments the left limits of your peripheral vision without shifting your forward focus; then notice for a few moments the right limits of your peripheral vision, again without shifting your forward focus. Finally, let your vision return to normal as you notice the wondrous sense of well-being and stillness within. Give yourself permission to experience that inner quietness to its fullest.

Step 3. Circular Touch. Bring the palms of your hands together and gently rub them against each other as you sense warm energy building between them. Separate your palms and use the tip of your right index finger to slowly form a circle in the palm of your left hand. Envision the circle and note the silken sensation as you slowly trace the circle several times with the tip of your right finger. Continue to trace the circle as you affirm: *I am now in full command of my life. I am energized, protected, and secure. I am fully empowered.*

Step 4. Empowerment Cue. Affirm in your own words your power to use the Circular Touch (Step 3) at any time as a cue to instantly activate the empowering effects of the full procedure.

You can use the circular touch cue at will as a powerful energizing and protection strategy, particularly in situations involving phobias and obsessive-compulsive reactions.

Day Four

Goal: To unleash subconscious growth resources that can fortify and protect the internal energy system against psychic vampirism.

Day four introduces two procedures designed to access and unleash subconscious resources required to successfully confront and vanquish psychic vampirism. The Hypno-liberation and Protection Procedure uses self-hypnosis to probe the vast, subconscious regions of the mind and uncover new insight and growth possibilities, with emphasis on functions that protect and defend us against psychic vampirism. The Sleep Protection Procedure places our subconscious resources in a state of readiness to repel any attempted invasion of psychic vampirism during sleep, while at the same time promoting peaceful, rejuvenating sleep and dreaming. The procedure requires approximately one hour during which there must be absolutely no distractions.

Hypno-liberation and Protection Procedure

Step 1. Goal Statement. Begin the procedure by settling back into a comfortable, relaxed position with legs uncrossed so as not to cut off circulation. Take a few moments to clearly formulate your empowerment goals, focusing particularly on those related to psychic vampirism. Examples are: (1) empowering your energy system to confront and defeat psychic vampirism, (2) discovering important insight, including past-life experiences relevant to psychic vampirism, and (3) initiating a powerful upward growth spiral. Specifically state your goals and affirm your intent to achieve them. Use imagery whenever possible to give substance to your stated goals.

Step 2. Eye Movement/Reverse Counting (EM/RC) Trance Induction Strategy. As you become increasingly comfortable and relaxed, close your eyes and give yourself permission to enter the trance state. Visualize yourself enveloped in a powerful sphere of bright energy as you affirm: *I am protected and secure as I now prepare to enter the trance state. Throughout this experience, I will be guided by my higher self and the higher cosmos.* With your eyes remaining closed, further affirm: *By counting slowly backward from 20 while moving my eyes from side-to-side with each count, I will go deeper and deeper into hypnosis. I will remain in full control throughout the trance experience. I can exit hypnosis at any time by simply deciding to do so.* With your eyes still closed, begin the trance by moving your eyes (without turning your head), first to your left on the count of 20, then to your right on the count of 19, then again to your left on the count of 18, and so forth. Accompany each side-to-side eye movement with a reverse count until you reach the count of 1. Upon the count of 1, let your eyes return to normal. Should you reach the desired trance state before the count of 1, discontinue the count and proceed to the next step.

Step 3. Deepening the Trance. You can deepen the trance as needed through any of the following procedures: (1) slowly counting again in reverse while interspersing suggestions of drowsiness and depth; (2) using suggestions to induce and then remove sensations such as numbness or tingling at selected body areas, including the hand or finger; and (3) using imagery of a peaceful nature scene, such as a tranquil lake, beach, or meadow, accompanied by suggestions of relaxation and drowsiness.

Step 4. Empowerment Applications. As you remain in the trance state, affirm your intent to experience the expansive domain of your subconscious with its wealth of resources. Visualize your conscious presence in that vast region as bright energy. As your experience that spacious part of yourself, let images and impressions unfold, a process that, at first, may seem similar to the dream experience. Affirm that the emerging experiences are an integral part of your being; and, as such, they are relevant to your present goals.

Step 5. Past-life Imagery. Remind yourself that your past-life experiences are relevant to your present growth, and give permission for them to gently unfold before you as clear images. Should a dark or threatening image emerge, illuminate it with the brightness of your presence rather than attempting to banish it. Think of each image as a source of knowledge and enlightenment, and allow it to become integrated into your total being. Affirm: *I am totally attuned and balanced to the subconscious part of my being.*

Step 6. Psychic Protection and Other Goals. Probe areas of subconscious darkness and illuminate them with bright energy. Illuminate any area of dark residue—including phobias and other anxiety states that feed on your energies—and let them become sources of insight and understanding rather than weights that impede your progress. Form bright images of your goals and let them become registered in your subconscious. For protection from psychic vampirism or any other threat to your well-being, visualize luminous energy permeating the deepest regions of your being and radiating outward to envelop you totally with a shield of bright energy. For other goals, visualize them in as much detail as possible and affirm them as your personal destiny.

Step 7. Post-hypnotic Cue. Bring your hands together as a gesture to symbolize protection, attunement, and balance. Affirm that by simply bringing your hands together, you can at any moment activate the full empowerment effects of the trance experience.

Step 8. Conclusion. State your intent to exit hypnosis by counting forward from 1 to 5. Upon the count of 5, open your eyes and take a few moments to reflect on the trance experience.

Sleep Protection Procedure

Step 1. Pre-sleep Imagery. Immediately before falling asleep, clear your mind of active thought and allow peaceful images to spontaneously flow in and out of your mind. Select a particularly pleasant image, perhaps a nature scene such as a landscape at sunset, a waterfowl in flight, or a sail by moonlight. Take a few moments to focus your full attention on the image, noting such details as color, shape, and motion. Give special attention to the serenity the image evokes.

Step 2. Goal Formulation. As you become increasingly drowsy, shift your attention to your solar plexus region as the center of your internal energy system. Sense that energy center at the core of your innermost being. Sense the vibrant energy emanating from that center infusing your body and enveloping your total being with a powerful, protective shield. Affirm in your own words that as you sleep, you will be protected and secure from any threat of psychic vampirism. Visualize your subconscious as a vast region of inner light with power to repel instantly the dark forces of vampirism. Affirm that any attempted vampire invasion will be decisively met with radiant, luminous energy that will promptly drive it back. At this point, you may wish to formulate other goals and affirm your ability and intent to achieve them.

Step 3. Cosmic Protection. Sense your connection to the bright center of the cosmos; and affirm in your own words that, as you sleep, the highest powers of the cosmos will be your constant protection. Envision bright energy of cosmic origin melding with your own energies to fully saturate and energize you mentally, physically, and spiritually.

Step 4. Sleep. Shift your attention to the scene you visualized in Step 1, noting again such details as color, shape, and motion. Continue to focus on the scene until sleep ensues, typically within a few minutes.

Step 5. Awakening Empowerment. Upon awakening from sleep, sense again bright cosmic energy from the center of the cosmos melding with your own energy system to protect and empower you totally. Affirm: *I am energized, attuned, and balanced. I am at one with the cosmic source of pure energy. I am safe, secure, and protected. I am empowered to achieve my highest goals.*

Note: For long-term effectiveness, this procedure should be practiced at least twice weekly.

Day Five

Goal: To access higher cosmic planes of power through astral travel.

For today, we introduce Astral Cosmic Voyage, a procedure specifically designed to induce the out-of-body state and then through astral travel, to access higher cosmic planes of power. This is a critical point in our seven-day plan. Even with no previous practice in astral projection, you can experience through this flexible procedure the expansive empowerment effects of the out-of-body state. By visiting selected cosmic planes, you can access specialized cosmic resources and focus them on psychic protection as well as other specific goals. Astral Cosmic Voyage requires a comfortable setting with no distractions or interruptions.

Astral Cosmic Voyage

Step 1. Preparation. Settle back and generate a quiet state of well-being by taking in a few deep breaths and clearing your mind of active thought. With your eyes closed, visualize a glowing mist slowly enveloping your body and fully permeating it as your muscles, joints, and tendons become increasingly relaxed. Think of the mist as cosmic energy with power to energize and protect you mentally, physically, and spiritually. Note the wondrous sense of peace and well-being deep within. Affirm your intent to travel out of body to the astral realm, and invoke the protection of that dimension. At this point, you may wish to invite a familiar cosmic guide to be your traveling companion for the duration of your astral journey into the higher cosmos.

Step 2. Out-of-body Induction. Begin the out-of-body induction process by mentally affirming your intent to travel out of your body and into the cosmic realm with its bountiful resources and multiples planes of power. Concentrate on the astral part of your being—the part that is designed to survive your transition to the other side. Sense your spiritual essence, and get the feel of moving freely about as though your were separate and free from your body. (Some astral travelers at this point think of themselves as in discarnate form, that is, free from the corporeal body.) At this stage, you can facilitate the out-of-body process through relevant imagery. For instance, you can visualize yourself walking along a forest trail, in and out of the shadows of towering trees. As you note the intricate patchwork of light and shadows on the forest floor, think of the shadows as the representing physical reality and the light as representing spiritual reality. Finally emerging from the shadows of the forest and coming into a place of bright light, note your sense of freedom and separation from your physical body resting at a distance. With the forest and its shadows now behind, sense bright astral energy emanating from the higher cosmos fully enveloping you. Sense yourself as if in apparition form, detached from the physical and gently ascending. Allow plenty of time for full out-of-body awareness to unfold; then remind yourself that you can travel at will throughout the cosmos to interact with its various planes and draw power from them.

Step 3. Astral Travel. As you survey the cosmic realm, notice the many planes of color until a particularly bright plane commands your attention. Focus only on that plane, and let yourself be drawn to it. Once within the designated plane, linger there until you are fully bathed in its colorful radiance. Sense the plane's abundant energies merging with your own energy system to forge an enveloping sphere of armor sufficient to protect you from any vampire essence or entity. Let yourself become totally infused with the plane's special power. Once the interaction is complete, give yourself permission to visit other planes and engage their specialized powers. (Note: At this step, almost all astral travelers become aware of a spiritual presence that guides their interactions among the various cosmic planes.)

Step 4. The Return. Once the cosmic interaction is complete, turn your attention to the place of bright light near the forest where your out-of-body journey began. Give yourself permission to return to that place, and from there into the forest with its patchwork of shadows and light. Finally back into the presence of your physical body in its familiar setting, note the emerging sense of astral and physical harmony as you become spontaneously reunited with your body.

Step 5. Conclusion. To conclude the procedure, focus on you breathing as you sense again the wondrous peace and harmony permeating your innermost being. Briefly review your excursion into the higher cosmos, and sense yourself enveloped in the radiant, protective sphere of cosmic energy. Affirm: *I am enveloped and infused with powerful cosmic energy. I am fully protected and secure. I can repel at will the threat of psychic vampirism by simply envisioning myself enveloped in a protective sphere of bright cosmic energy.*

This procedure is flexible and can be easily modified to accommodate other out-of-body techniques. Through practice, you will find that entering the out-of-body state and traveling to selected destinations become increasingly easy and rewarding.

Day Six

Goals: To develop skill in programming and using the quartz crystal as an energizing and protection tool.

Day six of our plan involves one of the most powerful empowerment tools known—the quartz crystal. Fortunately, the crystal is highly receptive to programming, and it can be used for a near unlimited range of goals. Our use of the tool, of course, focuses on its capacity to energize and protect against psychic vampirism. The Crystal Protection Procedure as follows guides the selection, programming, and application process. The procedure can be used for a crystal already in your possession, or for a fresh crystal to be selected from an assortment.

Crystal Protection Procedure

Step 1. **Crystal Selection.** Begin by stating in your own words your goal of using the crystal in your effort to energize and protect your energy system. While reflecting on your stated goal, select a crystal that seems appropriate to your needs. When selecting a crystal from an assortment, slowly pass your hand, palm side down, over the assortment and note the crystal that seems to stand out from the assortment. Briefly hold the crystal in your hand and sense your interaction with it. If the selected crystal seems inappropriate to your needs, return it to the assortment and repeat the selection process until you find a suitable crystal.

Step 2. **Crystal Programming.** Programming the selected crystal is a two-fold process that includes both deprogramming (sometimes called "cleansing") and installing a new program. To deprogram the crystal, simply hold it briefly under cool running water while stroking it gently; and then place it on a towel to air dry. To install a new program, hold the crystal in your palm as you invite it in your own words to become your empowerment partner, and then affirm your goal: *My goal is to energize and protect my energy system. Together, we will achieve that goal. Our interaction will empower me to neutralize and defeat psychic vampirism in whatever its form or strategy.* (You may at this point program the crystal for other personal goals by simply stating your goals and inviting the crystal to work with you in achieving them; however, a single crystal should be programmed for no more than three goals, preferably each of which is related.) To save the program, simply state: *Please stay.*

Step 3. Crystal Application. Once programmed, the crystal usually functions best when in close proximity to the physical body, such as when worn as an ornament or carried in your pocket, briefcase, or purse. You can enrich the crystal's functions by periodically stroking it while affirming your goals. For protection during sleep, the crystal can be situated on a bedside table or dresser.

Aside from its relevance to psychic vampirism, the procedure can be easily modified and used to achieve other personal goals.

Day Seven

Goal: To experience the limitless empowerment possibilities of the natural environment.

The final day of our seven-day plan celebrates the creative cosmic force that sustains our existence in the universe by introducing three simple procedures that incorporate three agents of nature—earth, tree, and star. Nowhere are the manifestations of cosmic power greater than in our natural surroundings. By interacting with the elements of nature, you can connect to the cosmos and experience energy in is purest, most powerful form. You can stimulate new growth and enrich your life with new possibilities for success and personal fulfillment. You can restore and revitalize your internal energy system. You can become balanced, attuned, and protected from all forms of psychic vampirism. Here are strategies that can connect you to the limitless empowerment resources of the higher cosmos.

Earth Interaction Procedure

The upper layer of the earth in which plants grow is critical to both plant life and our own physical existence; it is a resource for our total growth. In its simplest form, the Earth Interaction Procedure involves taking a handful of soil and grinding it gently between your hands as you sense its life-sustaining energies. Then, as you allow the soil to flow through your fingers, affirm that the energies of your being are merging with the abundant energies of the earth to fully balance and attune you to the highest cosmos. Peace of mind, a sense of well-being, and emotional security are invariably among the spin-off benefits of this procedure. As a footnote, I often incorporate this procedure into my clinical practice as a component of a therapeutic approach I call Earth Therapy, which recognizes the energizing and therapeutic effects of working with soil, particularly in the growing and nurturing of plants.

Tree Connection Procedure

To begin this procedure, select a tree that is especially appealing to you. A tree that seems to command your attention and invite your interaction is an excellent choice for this procedure. Upon choosing a tree, place your palms on its trunk and sense its energies. Think of the tree as a living antenna that connects your energy system to the higher cosmos. With your eyes closes, sense the infusion of cosmic energy, first in your palms and then throughout your total being. Conclude the exercise with a simple of expression of gratitude.

Star Interaction Procedure

Through this procedure, you can discover the law of fulfillment that binds you to the stars. Begin by viewing the night sky and selecting a particular star. Focus your full attention on the selected star as you note its position in the heavens and your sense of connection to it. After a few moments of contemplation, assign the star a name—any name that comes to mind. Think of the star as a cosmic creation and your contact to the greater cosmos. Call the star by name and affirm it as your cosmic partner. Turn your palms upward as you sense the star's bright energies interfusing your palms and flowing throughout your being—energizing, protecting, and connecting you to the great human star within yourself.

Summary

Equipped with the strategies presented in this plan, along with others found in this book, you have the essential tools and skills required for protection against psychic vampirism or any other threat to your well-being. Beyond that, you have all the resources you need for continued growth and enrichment. You can now take decisive action to achieve your personal goals and realize your highest potentials.

TEN

Conclusion

PSYCHIC VAMPIRISM IS alive and flourishing in the world today. While its existence spans centuries, it has never been more widespread nor its effects more profound. Whether one-on-one, group, parasitic, or global in form, psychic vampirism exacts a heavy toll—it demands energy and, as we have seen in some instances, it destroys lives. At a personal level, it wastes our energies and interrupts our growth. At a global level, it can literally drain the planet of its survival resources. It follows that finding ways of preventing psychic vampirism, or where it already exists, successfully encountering it, must be among our top priorities.

This book takes a very broad approach to the study of psychic vampirism. Anyone who lives by preying upon others can be seen as a psychic vampire. Any group or organization that exploits human beings meets the criteria for psychic vampirism. Abuse of human rights, "ethnic cleansing," narcotics trafficking, and organized crime have clear fingerprints of psychic vampirism on an alarming scale.

Reckless pollution of the environment, irresponsible disregard for threatened species, and exploitation of our natural resources are examples of global vampirism that affect everyone and, in some instances, literally put the future of the planet at risk. Aside from these is that vast category of parasitic vampirism that preys upon oneself.

Although my approach to the topic is broad, it identifies with precision the underlying concepts and dynamics of the phenomenon. It then develops step-by-step strategies that are now available to everyone to confront and overcome the threat of psychic vampirism, whatever its form. We can now discover anew our inner landscape and the power within ourselves. Equally as important, we can discover the cosmic landscape and become attuned to the life-force energies that sustain our existence—past, present, and future. Once interconnected and attuned, we have access to all the resources we need, whether within ourselves or in the outer cosmic realm. We can then achieve our highest destiny for growth and greatness—the ultimate goal of the concepts and strategies presented in this book.

In the end, our personal growth is an ongoing process demanding involvement of our total being. The following cardinal principles, once engraved in consciousness, can enrich that endless process:

- Accept yourself. Recognize your abilities as well as your limitations. Find ways of using your strengths to compensate for your weaknesses.

- Paint a larger canvas of your existence. Discover the rich scope of your interests, feelings, and abilities. Find ways of experiencing the infinite life force both within yourself and the higher cosmos.

- Bring the uncomfortable parts of your inner self to the surface. Face them and resolve them through self-understanding rather than self-condemnation.

- Embrace the ghosts of your past, including those found in the shadows of your past lives. Once you embrace them, you will find you no longer fear them.

▪ Replace fear with faith. According to St. Augustine, "Faith is to believe what you do not yet see; the reward for this faith is to see what you believe." Faith is a winged chariot that connects you to an unseen cosmic force beyond your fathoming. Through faith, you can fly over any obstacle and overcome any threat.

▪ Renounce self-contempt, self-destruction, self-hate, and self-underestimation. They are morbid cloak-and-dagger vampires that can strangle and suffocate.

▪ Be realistic (and tolerant) in your demands of yourself and your expectations of others. Personal growth is imperfect, uneven, incomplete, and sometimes slow and perplexing. The demand of extreme perfection is not heaven-sprung. It puts arrows in the vampire quiver of guilt.

▪ Become involved in helping others. Every act of kindness, compassion, and generosity is empowering, not only to others, but to yourself as well.

▪ Stay productively connected. The world is diverse yet interconnected and mutually interdependent. By banishing encumbering psychic vampirism, we can move closer to productive connectedness, tolerance, involvement, understanding, and universal personhood.

Glossary

abusive relationship. A couples relationship in which one partner, the abuser, disregards the feelings, rights, and wishes of the abused partner.

academic vampirism. Organized psychic vampirism found in the academic setting. See *organizational vampirism.*

addictive vampire. The psychic vampire usually preoccupied with reliving past vampire episodes and planning future conquests.

age regression. A hypnotic procedure in which one experiences past events involving one's present lifetime.

ambivalent vampire. The inexperienced vampire who struggles for liberation from vampirism while depending on the supportive energy of others.

Antennae Activation Strategy. A procedure designed to bring the internal energy system into a state of complete congruence with the outer cosmic system.

antisocial vampire. The psychic vampire with a long history of disregarding or violating the rights of others.

arranged relationship. A couples relationship typically built on certain situational factors, such as convenience and economics.

Astral Cosmic Voyage. A procedure designed to induce the out-of-body state, and then, through astral travel, to access higher cosmic planes of power.

astral projection. The experience of being in a spatial location outside the physical body with consciousness intact. Also known as out-of-body experience (OBE), astral travel, or soul travel.

aura. An external energy phenomenon enveloping all living things. See **human aura.**

Aura Hand-viewing Procedure. A procedure designed for viewing one's own aura.

Aura Liberation Procedure. A procedure designed to energize the constricted aura, while replacing discoloration and clusters of darkness with luminous energy.

Aura Orientation and Training. A program used in couples counseling to promote problem solving and mastery of appropriate aura intervention and protection strategies.

aura photography. Any procedure that photographs the aura. See **Kirlian photography.**

Aura Self-protection Massage. A procedure designed to exercise the aura and activate its internal defense powers.

biological genotype. Each individual's genetic makeup.

codependent relationship. A couples relationship in which both partners are dependent upon each other.

clairvoyance. Psychic perception of spatially distant realities. See **extrasensory perception.**

competitive relationship. A couples relationship built usually on the ego needs of partners for success, recognition, status, and wealth.

Corridor of Power. A strategy designed to counteract parasitic vampire tendencies and activate the self's coping and protection potentials.

Cosmic Color Procedure. A procedure designed to energize the full aura while applying concentrated masses of colorful cosmic energy to specific areas.

cosmic energy system. The energy system that exists throughout the known universe and beyond.

cosmic congruency. A state in which the internal energy system is brought into a state of congruency with the cosmic energy system. See *Antennae Activation Strategy.*

cosmic genotype. Each individual's unique cosmic makeup which remains unchanged from life to life and beyond.

Cosmic Protection Procedure. A procedure designed to balance, attune, and connect the aura to the cosmos through mind-over-aura intervention.

Crystal Protection Procedure. A procedure that uses the quartz crystal to energize and protect the human energy system.

cyberspace vampire. The experienced socialized psychic vampire who uses the Internet as a vampire tool.

dependent relationship. A couples relationship in which one partner is emotionally insecure and overly dependent on the other.

depersonalization. A sense of detachment from one's mind and body. See *parasitic vampirism.*

Earth Interaction Procedure. A procedure that uses interactions with soil as a personal empowerment resource.

Electra complex. In psychoanalysis, the female child's attraction to her father.

Energy Activation Procedure. A procedure designed to promote a fully functional internal energy system that meets mental, physical, and spiritual energy needs.

EM/RC technique. A trance induction procedure using certain eye movement and reverse counting strategies.

energy defense potential. The capacity of the internal energy system to repel any invading force, including psychic vampirism.

ESP. See *extrasensory perception.*

extrasensory perception (ESP). Perception occurring independently of sensory mechanisms or processes.

Finger Interlock Procedure. An aura protection procedure designed to erect a shield of energy around the full aura. See *halo effect.*

Global Empowerment Procedure. A group activity designed to generate energy sufficient to energize the earth and repel the forces of global vampirism.

global vampirism. Psychic vampirism on a massive, global scale.

Group Empowerment Procedure. A group procedure designed to organize group energies, infuse the group with new energy, and protect the group from psychic vampirism or other enfeebling influences.

group psychic vampirism. A collective form of psychic vampirism often found among informal groups as well as structured organizations and institutions.

halo effect. An outer ring of energy enveloping the human aura.

Handclasp of Power. A procedure designed to energize, repair, and protect the human energy system by opening up new energy pathways.

human aura. The human body's external energy field which is believed to be a manifestation of the internal energy system's central core.

Hypno-liberation and Protection Procedure. A self-hypnosis procedure designed to unleash subconscious growth resources.

hypno-production. A trance state in which totally new, highly developed skills emerge.

hypnosis. A trance state in which receptivity to suggestion is heightened.

Interaction Interview Guide. A questionnaire designed to measure the frequency of vampire-like social interactions.

Interaction Questionnaire IR. A test designed to measure the tendency toward one-on-one psychic vampirism in one's relationship with people in general.

Interaction Questionnaire IIR. A test designed to measure the tendency toward one-on-one psychic vampirism in one's relationship with a particular partner.

internal energy system. The energy system that exists within the self.

Kirlian photography. An electrophotographic process designed to record the aura.

luminous cluster phenomenon. A cluster of very bright energy occurring in the aura within the area or normal activity.

narcissistic vampire. A psychic vampire with a grandiose sense of self-importance along with needs for attention and admiration.

OBE. See *astral projection.*

Oedipus complex. In psychoanalysis, the male child's attraction to his mother.

one-on-one psychic vampirism. Any form of psychic vampirism between two persons, the one being the psychic vampire and the other the host victim.

Orb of Power. A versatile group procedure that uses the crystal ball as a tool for energizing and protecting individuals and the group as well for empowering the globe.

organizational psychic vampirism. A phenomenon in which psychic vampirism becomes so rampant and ingrained that an entire organization or institution acquires serious vampire traits.

out-of-body experience. See *astral projection.*

paranoid vampire. The psychic vampire who is suspicious and distrustful.

Parasitic Replacement Strategy. A strategy designed to target and replace specific parasitic vampire agents with an empowered state of well-being.

parasitic vampirism. An internal form of psychic vampirism turned against the self.

past-life regression. A hypnosis procedure in which one experiences past events occurring in one's past lifetimes. See *age regression.*

Perfect Relationship. A couples relationship in which partners are in denial regarding flaws in the relationship.

Peripheral Gaze Procedure. A procedure for viewing the aura. See *white-out effect.*

post-hypnotic cue. A cue presented during hypnosis that can later be used to instantly activate the effects of the trance.

precognition. The ESP of future events.

pre-incarnate life. Existence before one's first incarnation.

preliminary vampire maneuver. A common strategy used by one-on-one psychic vampires in initiating the vampire episode.

psychic empowerment perspective. A positive approach that recognizes the incomparable worth of each human being as a life-force entity with limitless possibilities for growth, change, and personal fulfillment.

psychic vampirism. The condition and practice of being a psychic vampire as well as the concepts associated with various forms of the phenomenon.

PV Self-rating Scale. An objective test designed to measure parasitic vampire tendencies.

Pyramid Empowerment Procedure. A multifunctional procedure that uses the pyramid to protect and empower the internal energy system.

relational continuity. A phenomenon in which highly meaningful past-life relationships continue beyond death to re-emerge in future lives.

remote image phenomenon. A small point of glowing energy occurring outside the normal range of activity in the aura.

schizoid vampire. The psychic vampire who tends to be socially withdrawn and uncomfortable except during the vampire episode.

self-hypnosis. A self-induced trance state in which one's receptivity to suggestion is heightened.

shadow phenomenon. A shadowy outer region enveloping the aura accompanied by unusually long tentacles that reach beyond the normal aura boundary.

Sleep Protection Procedure. A procedure designed to promote peaceful, rejuvenating sleep and dreaming while placing subconscious anti-vampire resources in a state of readiness.

socialized vampire. A socially skilled psychic vampire who, on the surface, appears to be trustworthy, friendly, cooperative, and responsible.

Star Interaction Procedure. A procedure that uses interactions with a selected star as a personal empowerment strategy.

Stress Reduction Response. A proactive procedure designed to eliminate negative stress and replace it with positive self-perceptions.

telepathy. Mind-to-mind communication. See *extrasensory perception.*

theistic spirituality. The view that human beings have an eternal spirit and that God communicates with them through spiritual channels.

Tree Interaction Procedure. A procedure that uses interaction with a selected tree as a personal empowerment strategy.

vampire. A creature of darkness who leaves the grave by night to suck the blood of the living.

vampire foreplay. A preliminary procedure commonly used by psychic vampires to reduce resistance of the selected host victim.

vampire infiltration. An organized, collective activity in which a psychic vampire subgroup is strategically positioned within a group to extract energy from the larger group.

vampire surfing. A phenomenon in which experienced psychic vampires survey a group and draw small amounts of energy from large numbers of people.

white-out effect. An optical illusion associated with aura viewing in which a glow enveloping the physical body precedes the emergence of the visible aura. See *Peripheral Gaze Procedure.*

Suggested Reading

Anderson, E. (1990). *Streetwise: Race, Class, and Change in an Urban Community.* Chicago: University of Chicago Press.

Ajzen, L., and M. Fishbein. (1980). *Understanding Attitudes and Predicting Social Behavior.* Englewood Cliffs, N.J.: Prentice-Hall.

Buss, D. (1994). *The Evolution of Desire.* New York, N.Y.: Basic Books.

Cialdini, R. (1993). *Influence, Science and Practice,* 3rd ed. New York, N.Y.: HarperCollins.

Cumes, D. (1999). *The Spirit of Healing.* St. Paul, Minn.: Llewellyn.

Damasio, A. (1999). *The Feeling of What Happens: Body and Emotion in the Making of Consciousness.* San Diego, Calif.: Harcourt Brace.

Donald, M. (1991). *Origins of the Modern Mind.* Cambridge, Mass.: Harvard University Press.

Eimer, B., and A. Freeman. *Pain Management Psychotherapy: A Practical Guide.* London: Wiley.

235

Erdelys, M. H. (1996). *The Recovery of Unconscious Memories*. Chicago: University of Chicago Press.

Farley, J. (1992). *Sociology*. Englewood Cliffs, N.J.: Prentice-Hall.

Freedy, J. R., and S. E. Hobfoll. (Eds.). (1995). *Traumatic Stress*. New York, N.Y.: Plenum.

Finley, G. (1999). *Design Your Destiny: Shape Your Future in 12 Easy Steps*. St. Paul, Minn.: Llewellyn.

Handy, C. (1994). *The Age of Paradox*. Cambridge, Mass.: Harvard Business School Press.

Herman, J. (1992). *Trauma and Recovery*. New York, N.Y.: Basic Books.

Kagan, J. (2000). *Three Seductive Ideas*. Cambridge, Mass.: Harvard University Press.

Klubertans, G. (1955). *Introduction to the Philosophy of Being*. New York, N.Y.: Appleton-Century-Crofts.

Liebman, J. (1946). *Peace of Mind*. New York, N.Y.: Simon & Schuster.

Loehle, C. (1996). *Thinking Strategically*. New York, N.Y.: Cambridge University Press.

Madanes, C. (1990). *Sex, Love, and Violence*. New York, N.Y.: Norton.

Nucho, A. O. (1995). *Spontaneous Creative Imagery: Problem Solving and Life Enhancing Skills*. Springfield, Ill.: Thomas.

———. (1988). *Stress Management: The Quest for Zest*. Springfield, Ill.: Thomas.

Ogilvie, R., and J. Harsh (Eds.). (1994). *Sleep Onset: Normal and Abnormal Processes*. Washington, D.C.: American Psychological Association.

Ornstein, R. (1992). *The Evolution of Consciousness*. Englewood Cliffs, N.J.: Prentice Hall.

Paulson, G. L. (1999). *Energy Focused Meditation: Body, Mind, Spirit*. St. Paul, Minn.: Llewellyn.

Pinker, S. (1999). *How the Mind Works*. New York, N.Y.: Norton.

Richards, S., and A. Bergin. (2000). *A Spiritual Strategy for Counseling and Psychotherapy*. Washington, D.C.: American Psychological Association.

Rieber, R. W. (1997). *Manufacturing Stress: Psychopathy in Everyday Life*. New York, N.Y.: Plenum.

Rose, N. (1996). *Inventing Ourselves*. New York, N.Y.: Cambridge University Press.

Segal, N. L., G. E. Weisfeld, and C. C. Weisfeld (Eds.). (1997). *Uniting Psychology and Biology*. Washington, D.C.: American Psychological Association.

Seligman, M. (1990). *Learned Optimism*. New York, N.Y.: Alfred A. Knopf.

Slate, J. H. (2001). *Rejuvenation: Strategies for Living Younger, Longer and Better*. St. Paul, Minn.: Llewellyn.

———. (1999). *Aura Energy for Health, Healing and Balance*. St. Paul, Minn.: Llewellyn.

———. (1998). *Astral Projection and Psychic Empowerment: Techniques for Mastering the Out-of-body Experience*. St. Paul, Minn.: Llewellyn.

———. (1996). *Psychic Empowerment for Health and Fitness*. St. Paul, Minn.: Llewellyn.

———. (1995). *Psychic Empowerment: A Seven-day Plan for Self Development*. St. Paul, Minn.: Llewellyn.

Tannen, D. (1994). *Gender and Discourse*. New York, N.Y.: Oxford.

Welch, P. (1999). *The Energy Body Connection: The Healing Experience of Self-embodiment*. St. Paul, Minn.: Llewellyn.

Wilson, C. (1999). *After Life; Survival of the Soul*. St. Paul, Minn.: Llewellyn.

Young, G. D. (1997). *Adult Development, Therapy, and Culture: A Postmodern Synthesis*. New York, N.Y.: Plenum.

Index